SPECIAL SUBSCRIBER'S EDITION

INVESTING IN

Small-CAP STOCKS

BLOOMBERG PRESS
PRINCETON

Special Abridged Edition for the subscribers to
Bloomberg Personal magazine.

Chart illustrations by Myra Klockenbrink.
Diamond icon illustration by Natasha Tibbott.

Book design by Don Morris Design

*To Jennifer and Claire,
for their love, friendship, and encouragement*
—C.G.

ACKNOWLEDGMENTS

THIS BOOK HAS BEEN A LOT OF FUN to write, thanks to the support and enthusiasm of countless people. Here's where my coauthor and I get to actually say thanks to a few of them.

From concept through research, writing, and revising, Bill Inman, who manages the magazine and publishing group, has given us his complete support and nearly unlimited resources to produce the best book we could. That task was made easier by the fact that we work for an organization and a boss as well respected as Bloomberg Financial Markets and Mike Bloomberg, whose name opened doors and data banks for us. Among the market professionals who answered our questions, offered ideas, and provided research and charts, we owe a particular debt to Bill Berger, founder of the Berger Funds; Mike Berry at Heartland Advisors; Dan Coker at Schroders; Michael Gerding of Founders Funds; Roger Ibbotson of Ibbotson Associates; Steve Kim at Merrill Lynch; Claudia Mott at Prudential Securities; Bill Nasgovitz of Heartland Advisors; Steve Norwitz at T. Rowe Price; Jim Oberweis Jr. of Oberweis Funds; Satya Pradhuman at Merrill Lynch; Robert Rodriguez of First Pacific Advisors; Tom Dorsey of Dorsey, Wright & Assoc.; Chuck Royce of Quest Advisory; John Spears of Tweedy, Browne Co.; and Matt Wright at First Investors.

A WORD FROM THE PUBLISHER

I HOPE YOU ENJOY this special subscriber's edition of *Investing in Small-Cap Stocks*. About two years ago, two of our senior editors, Chris Graja and Betsy Ungar, sat down to write an article on small-cap stocks for Bloomberg's magazine for market professionals. What they found is that there is very little written about this class of assets, which has historically returned more than almost any other investment available to individual investors.

This special edition focuses on sophisticated strategies, rather than the fundamentals, which are the core of the full-length book. One theme that runs through the sections that were edited out of this special edition is that risk is your constant companion when you are investing in small caps. Although greed may tempt you to place big bets on small caps or fear may tempt you to avoid them completely, we feel that it is a more prudent strategy for long-term investors to make small caps one portion of a portfolio that includes large stocks, bonds, international investments, and short-term securities like Treasury bills.

I sincerely hope you enjoy this special edition, and will seek out the full-length book, *Investing in Small-Cap Stocks*, to help you become an expert investor. As a subscriber to *Bloomberg Personal* you will have the opportunity to learn a lot more about small caps through the authors' regular coverage of the market and Bloomberg's exclusive Internet page.

Michael R. Bloomberg

C O N T E N T S

Introduction

THIS IS A NO-NONSENSE guide to making money. It's for long-term investors, not speculators, people who want to beat inflation but aren't willing to stake their life's savings on the slim chance of making a killing. And the best way I know to achieve superior returns with reasonable risk is to put part of your savings into stocks having small market capitalizations—companies like the Scotts Co. and Vans, Inc., whose issued shares have market values that are dwarfed by those of IBM and Microsoft.

You probably already know that in the long run, stocks beat out investments like bonds and money markets. You may also have heard that small stocks trounce larger ones. If not, here are a few stats to convince you: According to a study by Chicago-based consultants Ibbotson Associates (whose findings are summarized in the charts on pages 4 through 7), stocks outperformed bonds in every one of the 20-year periods from 1926 to 1995, and in 94 percent of those periods, the smallest stocks did better than larger ones. Twenty years is probably a suitable investment horizon for most working people. But even if you're retired and most of your biggest bills lie behind you, you may well need to keep your savings growing for another 10 years or more. So you should know that Ibbotson also concluded that stocks beat out bonds in 86 percent of the 10-year periods between 1926 and 1995, and the smallest stocks outshone all other investments in 60 percent of those periods.

With comparisons like that, why am I telling you to put just part of your savings in small stocks? Why not the whole wad? Because, as you probably also know, there's no free lunch. Higher returns come with greater risks. That's the curse of an efficient market.

Investors in U.S. Treasury bills, notes, and bonds may barely beat inflation, but they know if they hold on to their securities till maturity, they'll get their principal back; equity investors can lose their shirts. In addition, the small-cap performance figures quoted above have been averaged over a 70-year period, a process that smooths out some heavy-duty price volatility and variability. During certain months, years, even decades, the small-stock group lagged giants like Intel Corp. and Nike.

20-YEAR ROLLING PERIOD RETURNS

TYPE	MAXIMUM VALUE	
	RETURN	YEARS
Small Company Stocks	21.13	1942–61
Large Company Stocks	16.86	1942–61
Long-Term Corporate Bonds	10.58	1976–95
Long-Term Government Bonds	10.45	1976–95
Intermediate-Term Government Bonds	9.85	1974–93
U.S. Treasury Bills	7.72	1972–91
Inflation	6.36	1966–85

And for the entire period, the triple-digit growth of a few stars pulled up a large number of stocks that went nowhere or failed altogether. Small companies, which often have only a few products and limited reserves against hard times, are particularly vulnerable to recessions, rising interest rates, or the loss of key executives; it takes only a few spooked investors to send their sparsely traded shares down the tube.

In short, small stocks are risky. Pick the wrong one or the wrong time to buy it, and you can kiss part of your nest egg goodbye. "Certainly in any

MINIMUM VALUE		TIMES POSITIVE (OUT OF 51 OVERLAPPING 20-YR PERIODS)	TIMES HIGHEST RETURNING ASSET
RETURN	YEARS		
5.74	1929–48	51	48
3.11	1929–48	51	3
1.34	1950–69	51	0
0.69	1950–69	51	0
1.58	1940–59	51	0
0.42	1931–50	51	0
0.07	1926–45	51	0

study that you ever read about how small caps have performed, you are going to see that you get that extra return," says Prudential Securities director of small-cap research Claudia Mott. "But it doesn't come without a lot of added risk. And, certainly, the smaller you get in size, the worse the risk tends to get."

The lesson is to be cautious, not afraid. Despite their volatility and principal imperilment, these investments are still your best buffer against what Bill Wilson, economist at Comerica Bank, has characterized as the real danger facing low-saving

10-YEAR ROLLING PERIOD RETURNS

TYPE	MAXIMUM VALUE	
	RETURN	YEARS
Small Company Stocks	30.38	1975–84
Large Company Stocks	20.06	1949–58
Long-Term Corporate Bonds	16.32	1982–91
Long-Term Government Bonds	15.56	1982–91
Intermediate-Term Government Bonds	13.13	1982–91
U.S. Treasury Bills	9.17	1978–87
Inflation	8.67	1973–82

Americans: having to spend their underfunded golden years flipping burgers under the Golden Arches. Small stocks have offered better returns over the past 70 years than any investment except loans to new businesses. You need the kind of reward they offer to reach your long-range goals. And you can reduce the risks that go with it by just planning your portfolio properly, doing a bit of homework, and sticking to a few well-thought-out strategies. That's what this book is about.

In the following chapters my coauthor, Elizabeth Ungar, and I will explain how to incorporate the

| MINIMUM VALUE | | TIMES POSITIVE (OUT OF 61 | TIMES HIGHEST |
RETURN	YEARS	OVERLAPPING 10-YR PERIODS)	RETURNING ASSET
-5.70	1929–38	59	35
-0.89	1929–38	59	16
0.98	1947–56	61	6
-0.07	1950–59	60	0
1.25	1947–56	61	2
0.15	1933-42/1934–43	61	1
-2.57	1926–35	55	1

high performance of small stocks into your portfolio without high anxiety. The exact method you choose will depend on what kind of investor you are. You might feel most comfortable, for example, leaving the detailed decisions to a professional. In that case, you would probably do all your small-cap investing through mutual funds. A good fund manager can earn you returns of 15 percent a year. That's after expenses, which can be steep—usually about 1 to 2 percent of the assets you invest. But doing it right yourself isn't cheap, either: One percent of a $100,000 investment is $1,000, which disappears pretty fast when you start buying a souped-up computer and subscribing to a few periodicals. And that doesn't count the time you need to spend.

On the other hand, you might be someone who likes to take matters into your own hands. You should still probably put a large part of your small-cap portfolio into funds. But you might want to devote a small portion to individual stocks, picking

and following these yourself or with the help of a broker specializing in the small-cap market.

Whichever route you choose, this book will help you on your way with information, advice, and strategies—all of it supplied by experts in the field and expressed whenever possible in their own words. (One cautionary note: A disadvantage of letting people speak their own minds is that you also allow them to cite their own pet statistics; as a result, the same point made in different places in the book may be bolstered by different data, none necessarily inaccurate, just derived from diverse time periods or sets of securities.)

The full-length book was written for a range of readers, from relative market novices to those who, though not professionals, have experience with stocks and perhaps have dabbled in derivatives. Since this special edition is aimed at the sophisticated investor, less-experienced investors should carefully read the first chapter to ensure they have the background they need at each stage to apply the recommendations and schemes described.

The one ground rule is to enjoy yourself. Sure, investing, by definition, means giving up something: stuff you won't allow yourself to spend money on right now, time you have to devote to tending your nest egg. But don't let it drive you nuts. A reporter once asked professional golfer Tom Kite (at the time, the PGA tour's all-time money winner) how he dealt with the pressure of a putt on which several hundred thousand dollars were riding. He answered that having the chance to win that much money wasn't a burden; it was the culmination of everything he'd worked for. We all dream of being able to do something to make life better for our families. You should feel good about investing. Just by doing it, you're miles ahead of the rest of the world.

CHRISTOPHER GRAJA

CHAPTER 1

Laying the Foundation

SUCCESSFUL INVESTING has two components. One is finding areas where you have an edge and putting your money there. The other is integrating the investments you make into a diverse portfolio that has been constituted to reflect both your long- and short-term savings goals.

In this chapter, you'll see that the small-cap sector is one area in which an individual investor can find an edge—where, in fact, small players have distinct advantages over large institutions. You'll learn, as well, how small stocks fit into a general investment strategy, both boosting the returns of your portfolio and reducing their variability. Along the way, I'll slip in a few definitions of concepts that you will need to understand in order to apply the tips and advice given later.

A Small Cap Is Not a Beanie

"I would tell every individual investor not to spend a whole lot of time analyzing Coca-Cola. If they're going to put their efforts on something and do stock analysis, it should be in the micro-cap, small-cap area."
— JOHN MARKESE, president of the American Association of Individual Investors, during a February 1996 episode of "Adam Smith's Money World"

YOU'VE PROBABLY GOT THE IDEA by now that small-cap companies can be a good investment. But what exactly are they? To understand, you have to know that *cap* is shorthand for *market capitalization*, which refers to the market value of a company's common stock. It is equal to the number of shares outstanding times the price per share. So a small-cap company is one that either has issued only a few shares or trades at a low price in the market. It may not be diminutive by any other measure—sales, assets, staff though just about everyone in the field, including me, uses small stock, small company, and small cap interchangeably.

Microsoft, which has 597.6 million shares outstanding, each priced, as of November 1996, at $150.50, is obviously a large-cap stock; fast-food franchiser Nathan's Famous, with 4.7 million $3 shares, is just as indisputably small. Somewhere in between lies the cutoff—exactly where depends on who's counting and whether the market as a whole has been growing or retrenching. Complicating matters, *non*large stocks are often subdivided into *mid-, small-,* and *microcap.*

The fluidity of the boundaries between all these categories is one reason analysts often refer not to dollar ranges but to *deciles* and *quintiles*—10- and 20-percent segments, respectively, of a universe of stocks ranked according to some criterion, such as market cap. That's a useful solution for academic studies that generalize across periods in which share prices and market size vary considerably. But for you and me, it's easier to talk in concrete dollars. So I settled on the following cutoffs, which more or less reflect the current consensus. When I say "small," I mean any stock with a capitalization less than $1 billion. I'll use "micro" only when

CUTOFFS USED IN THIS BOOK

Large Cap   ≥$3.5 Billion

Mid-Cap $1 Billion - $3.5 Billion

Small Cap
<$1 Billion

Microcap
<$250
Mil.

I need to distinguish the subset of small stocks having caps below $250 million. "Mid-cap" refers to stocks between $1 billion and about $3.5 billion in size; anything above that is "large." *(For a graphic representation of the cutoffs, see the diagram, left.)*

The smaller the cap size of the category, the more companies it contains, a fact captured by the major associated indexes *(illustrated in the chart below)*. A stock index provides a measure of the performance of a particular market segment using the combined weighted performances of a group of companies that are considered representative. Weightings are assigned according to various criteria, including capitalization, and members are replaced as their defining characteristics change. The index most commonly used as a proxy for the large-cap universe is the Standard & Poor's 500, which tracks a group of 500 companies that, as of June 1996, had a total market capitalization of more than $5 trillion. The Russell Mid-Cap Index has 800 members, but their combined market cap is only $2 trillion, 40 percent as large as that of the S&P. The cap of the Russell 2000, widely cited as a small-cap benchmark, is $804 billion, 16 percent of the

FOUR OF THE MAJOR INDEXES

NUMBER OF COMPANIES	S&P 500	COMBINED MARKET CAP
500 Companies		$5.0 Trillion
	RUSSELL MID-CAP	
800 Companies		$2.0 Trillion
	RUSSELL 2000	
2,000 Companies		$804 Billion
	CRSP 9-10	
3,331 Companies		$257 Billion

S&P's and equal to less than twice the assets under management of mutual fund company Fidelity Investments. The CRSP 9-10 index compiled by the Center for Research in Securities Prices contains 3,331 microcap stocks (in the 9th and 10th deciles) that weigh in at a tiny $257 billion in total market cap.

However you define them, small caps are profitable. According to data compiled by Chicago consulting firm Ibbotson Associates *(displayed in the table below)*, the little guys have outperformed the big ones by an average of 2 percent a year since 1926.

But bear in mind a couple of caveats. First, Ibbotson defined small-cap stocks for its survey as those in the lowest quintile in terms of market cap; in the 1990s, that would produce a cutoff of $155 million, well within my *microcap* category. In fact, it seems that much of the outperformance of the small-cap sector is produced by the very smallest, and riskiest, segment.

Second, the figures cited are averages. In each of the decades studied, a sizable number of small companies not only failed to grow at the rate shown in the chart but actually failed altogether. Of course, those failures mean at least a few other stocks far outstripped the average.

To see how variable the results of a small-cap portfolio—even one put together by well-informed experts—can be, consider the one-year results for *Individual Investor* magazine's "Magic 25." This is a portfolio of 25 very small stocks that the magazine's market-savvy editors believe have tremendous growth potential. Accord-

RETURNS FOR LARGE AND SMALL CAPS*

	1920s	'30s	'40s	'50s
Small	-4.5	1.38	20.69	16.9
Large	19.9	-.05	9.17	19.35

* "SMALL CAPS"= STOCKS IN THE LOWEST TWO DECILES IN TERMS OF MARKET CAP

ing to the table appearing in the January 1997 issue, the portfolio as a whole rose 15.7 percent in 1996. Individual stock performance, however, ranged from a 372 percent gain for Act Networks to a 99.2 percent *loss* for Vista 2000.

Bob Barker—the "Warren Buffett of small-cap stocks," according to "Adam Smith's Money World"—feels the sector's extreme variability can work to investors' benefit. The octogenarian head of the investment firm Barker Lee & Co. pointed out in a February 1996 "Money World" appearance that "if... half your companies are mistakes, and you lose everything in them, and the other half go up between 5 and 10 times, that's all you need." Barker tested this insight by putting together a theoretical portfolio of 20 companies and leaving it alone for five years. At the end of that time, nine stocks had fallen, four of them by 80 to 90 percent. But the portfolio as a whole had an annual compound rate of return of 23 percent, because the winners had risen between 80 and about 1,000 percent.

Barker's point was illustrated in a family story told by Bill Sams, manager of the First Pacific Advisors Paramount fund, at the 1996 conference sponsored by Morningstar Mutual Funds, the Chicago rating service. "My father bought $700 worth of Frito in the old days," Sams said. "Frito got bought out by Lay's, and then Lay's got bought by Pepsi. That investment turned into more than $6 million. Every other stock he bought lost money, but that one made up for it."

'60s	'70s	'80s	'90s	AVG	$1.00 INVESTED IN 1926
15.53	11.49	15.83	11.47	12.2	$2,843
7.81	5.86	17.55	11.53	10.19	$811

Where's the Edge?

"There was a two-tier market: You had large companies selling at 20 times earnings, and small companies with prospects similar to large companies selling at 12 times earnings. There seemed to be a lot more value in the smaller companies, so I learned that way. And back then there were a lot of small companies not followed by analysts. You could call on somebody and get information that had not been widely published."

— RALPH WANGER, manager of Acorn Fund, telling *Kiplinger's Personal Finance Magazine* in a February 1995 interview why he started his small-cap fund in the 1970s

VALUATION VS. COMPANY SIZE & GROWTH RATE

Small and midsize growth companies are cheaper than large growth companies, relative to expected earnings per share.

	AVG. MARKET CAP (S MILLION)	QUINTILE BY MARKET CAP
Large	$ 14,036.89	1
Mid	1,590.05	2
Small	641.37	3
Small	307.14	4
Micro	123.76	5

◆ SAMPLE—1,272 U.S. COMPANIES AS OF DECEMBER 31, 1996. ◆ P/E BASED ON CONSENSUS 12-MONTH FORWARD EPS ESTIMATE. ◆ LONG-TERM GROWTH = PROJECTED FIVE-YEAR EPS GROWTH RATE. ◆ COMPANIES IN SAMPLE INCLUDE

NOW THE REALLY IMPORTANT QUESTION: Why are stocks with small market capitalizations particularly good for individual investors like you? The answer: Although things have changed since the early days of Acorn to which Ralph Wanger was referring, you still have a better chance of finding real value in small stocks than in larger ones.

First, as the table below illustrates, the prices at which small companies trade are generally lower in relation to their expected earnings growth than those of larger companies. I'll discuss the price-to-earnings ratio later, in the section on growth and value, but for now, you should know that this measure indicates that the smallest stocks, as a group, deliver the best value.

Second, more good values exist among these com-

AVERAGE P/E RATIO				
28.46	21.07	18.69	16.05	13.53
28.08	17.68	15.98	13.66	12.42
23.99	16.78	14.57	11.77	11.89
21.20	16.04	12.49	11.88	12.69
17.69	12.61	11.48	11.04	11.56
1	2	3	4	5

QUINTILE BY LONG-TERM EPS GROWTH

Fastest Expected Growth ← → *Slowest Expected Growth*

32.25	21.20	16.05	12.38	7.88

AVERAGE LONG-TERM EPS GROWTH

ONLY THOSE SHOWING POSITIVE INCREASING EARNINGS FOR 1996, 1997 (PROJECTED), AND 1998 (PROJECTED), WITH MARKET CAPITALIZATION IN EXCESS OF $50 MILLION, AND WITH SHARE PRICE ABOVE $5.

SOURCE: T. ROWE PRICE ASSOCIATES, INC.

panies because so many of the big players give the sector short shrift. It's a matter of economics: Large institutional investors can't earn enough on small stocks to recover their research costs. An institution must know a lot about a company to feel comfortable buying a stake in it. That can take many hours of a researcher's high-priced time and probably an on-site visit. Any purchase the institution makes must have the potential to boost its returns enough to cover these expenses and then some. But to move a $10 billion portfolio requires an investment of at least $100 million. That would amount to 10 percent of a company with a market cap of $1 billion. Many portfolio managers are limited by their mandates to 5 percent stakes. Even those not so limited might find it impossible or imprudent to amass a large number of shares of small-cap companies, which generally trade infrequently, in small blocks, and among a limited number of buyers and sellers.

Brokerages also neglect small stocks, as illustrated in the bar graph *(below)*. Although the 450 U.S. companies with market caps larger than $2.4 billion are covered by an average of 22 analysts each, according to Merrill Lynch, the 2,600 companies between $60 million and $600 million are each followed by about three: "the underwriter, the co-underwriter, and usually the third is a total fool," jokes a money manager at a New

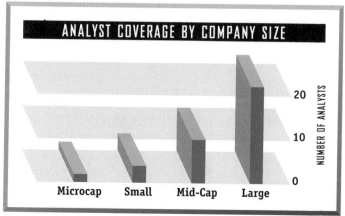

ANALYST COVERAGE BY COMPANY SIZE

NUMBER OF ANALYSTS

20

10

0

Microcap   Small   Mid-Cap   Large

SOURCE: MERRILL LYNCH QUANTITATIVE ANALYSIS, I/B/E/S

York–based mutual fund. The even tinier microcap issues average about two analysts each; it's your guess if the dropout is the co-underwriter or the fool.

The reasons for this neglect are again economic. "It does not pay [a broker] to have an analyst research a company where a buy recommendation will not generate orders for hundreds of thousands of shares," investment advisor Tweedy, Browne Co. says in a February 1996 letter to its clients explaining why the firm likes the small sector.

The result: Many fine companies remain undetected, their share prices far below what their intrinsic value would justify. You—or the manager of a mutual fund nimble enough to profit from small-cap research—gain an edge by discovering these gems before other investors can bid them up.

Finding them, moreover, does not take a jeweler's loupe. Again according to Tweedy, smaller companies are often easier to analyze than larger ones: They tend to have fewer products and lower debt levels, since borrowing is more difficult for them.

The relative simplicity of small caps means that the professionals' huge staffs and technical support give them less of an advantage over individuals here than in the large-cap sector. I once asked Peter Kris (managing director of the Van Wagoner funds and no relation to the drummer from Kiss) if an ordinary investor could replicate any part of the strategy followed by star small-stock picker Garrett Van Wagoner. "All of it," he said. "Garrett is just an individual investor who has decided to devote his life to it. He has no analysts and finds that he can uncover new developments before Wall Street analysts [do]."

All Part of a Grand Plan

"Two are better than one; because they have a good reward for their labour. / For if they fall, the one will lift up his fellow: but woe to him that is alone when he falleth; for he hath not another to help him up."
— ECCLESIASTES *4:9, 10*

SMALL-CAP STOCKS ARE A crucial investment if you want to get the most value out of your research and grow your wealth faster than inflation eats into it. But crucial as they are, they should still be just one part of a larger, diverse portfolio whose composition is determined by an overarching savings strategy.

The key word here is diverse. You never want to put all your eggs in one basket, whether it's one U.S. Treasury bond or a selection of Pacific Rim equities. Only by diversifying can you ensure both the growth you'll need for a prosperous future and protection against the economic and company-specific bumps you'll inevitably hit.

Your portfolio, of course, shouldn't look like your grandfather's (unless you're 75 and he's 110). Different goals, outlooks, and stages of life demand different investment classes in different proportions. The pie charts on the following pages show the asset allocations that experts typically recommend for the main stages of a person's financial life cycle. These are just guidelines. If you need pointers on modifying the mix to suit your particular needs, you should turn to a book such as Burton Malkiel's *A Random Walk Down Wall Street*, or go to www.russell.com, the Web site run by the same folks who compile the Russell 2000 index of small-cap stocks (see "Resources"). But whatever your stage in life and specific needs, the same general principle applies: To get good growth with a minimum of risk, you should divide your investments between debt and equity; your equities between large and small stocks; and your small stocks among different size, regional, and style segments.

Debt and Equity

"By mixing bonds with small stocks, a portfolio can have higher returns yet no greater volatility."
— PETER L. BERNSTEIN, author of *Against the Gods: The Remarkable Story of Risk*

NO MATTER HOW CAUTIOUS OR aggressive you are as an investor, your portfolio should contain both instruments that conserve principal and those that, in the long run, increase it. The prototypical principal conservators are government debt instruments such as Treasury bonds, bills, and notes; the standard growth producers are equities, or stocks. These two types of securities serve two distinct purposes. Treasuries are best for funding fast-approaching goals, since you know exactly how much money you'll have if you hold them until maturity. They provide a short-term cushion that allows you to put money you don't need immediately into stocks, whose earnings tend to be higher but more variable (see the graph on page 28). Stocks are used to beat inflation and ensure that you have the funds you need to meet expenses in the more-distant future.

Diversifying your investments thus enables you to provide for both imminent needs and far-off goals. It also serves to stabilize the value of your portfolio. Different types of investments tend to prosper in different economic climates, so while one part of a diversified portfolio is taking a breather, another may be coming on strong. Stocks and bonds, for instance, have moved in tandem in the recent period of economic growth with low inflation, but a change in either condition could send them careening in opposite directions. In a low-inflation recession, for instance, bonds might rally

TYPICAL RECOMMENDED ASSET ALLOCATIONS

AGE: Mid-Twenties

LIFESTYLE: Fast, aggressive. With a steady stream of earnings, capacity for risk is fairly high. Need discipline of payroll savings to build nest egg

CASH (5%): Money-market fund or short-term-bond fund (average maturity 1 to 1½ years)

BONDS (25%): Zero-coupon Treasury bonds; no-load GNMA fund; or no-load high-grade bond fund

STOCKS (70%): 20% small-company stock fund; 20% growth stock fund; 15% international stock fund; 15% growth and income or "value" fund

AGE: Mid-Fifties

LIFESTYLE: Many still reeling from college tuitions. No matter what the lifestyle, this age group must start thinking about retirement and the need for income protection

CASH (5%): Money-market fund or short-term-bond fund (average maturity 1 to 1½ years)

BONDS (45%): 10% zero-coupon Treasury bonds; 17½% no-load GNMA fund; 17½% no-load high-grade bond fund

STOCKS (50%): 10% international stock fund; 20% high-income stock fund; 20% growth and income or "value" fund

AGE: Late Thirties to Early Forties

LIFESTYLE: Midlife crisis. For childless career couples, capacity for risk is still quite high. Risk options vanishing for those with college tuitions looming

CASH (5%): Money-market fund or short-term-bond fund (average maturity 1 to 1½ years)

BONDS (35%): 10% zero-coupon Treasury bonds; 12½% no-load GNMA fund; 12½% no-load high-grade bond fund

STOCKS (60%): 10% small-company stock fund; 10% growth stock fund; 10% international stock fund; 30% growth and income or "value" fund

AGE: Late Sixties and Beyond

LIFESTYLE: Enjoying leisure activities but also guarding against major health costs. Little or no capacity for risk

CASH (10%): Money-market fund

BONDS (60%): 20% no-load short- or intermediate-term bond fund; 20% no-load GNMA fund; 20% no-load high-grade bond fund

STOCKS (30%): 15% high-income stock fund; 15% growth and income or "value" fund as stocks slump. An opposite reaction could follow an inflationary expansion. By holding both instruments, you position yourself to win either way. That's a lot safer, and cheaper, than trying to time the market, constantly jumping out of one period's losers and into its winners.

Large and Small

"I now favor investing in an index that contains a much broader representation of U.S. companies [than the S&P 500], including large numbers of dynamic companies that are likely to be in early stages of their growth cycles."
— BURTON G. MALKIEL,
in *A Random Walk Down Wall Street*

IT IS AS IMPORTANT TO diversify your equity holdings as it is to diversify your overall portfolio, and for the same reasons. By investing in both small and large stocks in a variety of industries, you stabilize your returns while also giving them a boost.

Just as equities as a class outpace bonds, the more volatile small stocks outperform slow-but-steadier large ones. This is illustrated in the graph *(right)*. Of course,

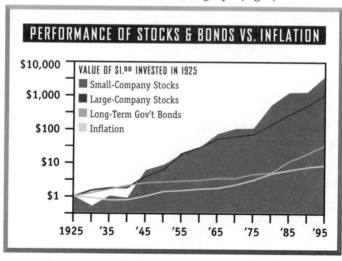

PERFORMANCE OF STOCKS & BONDS VS. INFLATION

VALUE OF $1.00 INVESTED IN 1925
■ Small-Company Stocks
■ Large-Company Stocks
Long-Term Gov't Bonds
Inflation

$10,000
$1,000
$100
$10
$1

1925 '35 '45 '55 '65 '75 '85 '95

SOURCE: CRSP; THE UNIVERSITY OF CHICAGO, PRUDENTIAL SECURITIES INC.

extra return usually involves extra risk. But time tends to reduce the trade-off. Statistics compiled by Ibbotson Associates illustrate this point. Ibbotson studied the 1-, 5-, 10-, 15-, and 20-year returns of government and corporate bonds and large and small stocks from 1926 through 1995, noting both the maximum and minimum values generated by each security type. The gap between the highest and lowest values decreases steadily as you move from risky small caps to conservative U.S. Treasury bills, but so does the size of the greatest gains: the one-year returns of small caps during this period ranged from 142.87 to –58.01; U.S. Treasury bills, meanwhile, earned from 14.71 to –0.02 annually. As the holding period lengthens, differences in variability decline while growth rates continue to diverge: The maximum and minimum 20-year returns for small stocks were 21.13 and 5.74 percent, respectively, versus 7.72 and 0.42 percent for T-bills.

Given those performance figures, small stocks can clearly play a specific role in your portfolio: funding goals that lie in the relatively distant future and that will require outlays well beyond your current cash reserves and income. For example, they're suited to saving for a far-off retirement or your baby's college tuition.

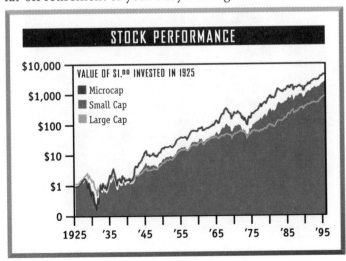

STOCK PERFORMANCE

VALUE OF $1.00 INVESTED IN 1925

■ Microcap
■ Small Cap
■ Large Cap

$10,000
$1,000
$100
$10
$1
0

1925   '35   '45   '55   '65   '75   '85   '95

Adding small caps to your investment mix also provides the second benefit of diversification: stable returns in a variety of environments. Small and large stocks, like equities and bonds, tend to perform best at different times and in response to different economic factors. "It is generally accepted that big-cap and small-cap stocks perform in alternating multiyear cycles," Kenneth Fisher and Joseph Toms, president and senior vice president of Fisher Investments, point out in the book *Small Cap Stocks*. These cycles of under- and overperformance *(discussed more fully in the next chapter)* last anywhere from three to more than seven years.

In addition, smaller companies generally react more quickly to changes in the economy than larger ones, according to Susan Belden, senior editor of the newsletter *No-Load Fund Analyst*. Because of their extra sensitivity, small stocks will outperform large ones at the beginning of an economic recovery and underperform when recession is looming.

Different-size companies also respond differently to inflation. When the rate is rising, nimble businesses that have near monopolies in fast-growing niches generate better earnings than more unwieldy corporations

RISK/RETURN: SMALLER STOCKS VS. LARGE

ANNUALIZED TOTAL RETURN*

14.1% — 10% Microcap, 90% Large
13.9
13.7 — 10% Mid-cap, 90% Large
13.5
13.3
13.1 — 10% Small, 90% Large
12.9
12.7 — 100% Large Cap

VOLATILITY (ANNUALIZED STANDARD DEVIATION)

15.10%   15.15   15.20   15.25   15.30

The results of adding micro-, mid-, and small-cap stocks to a 100% large-cap portfolio

*1/74-6/96

SOURCE: MERRILL LYNCH QUANTITATIVE ANALYSIS

operating in broader, highly competitive markets. And better earnings translate into higher stock prices. In his book, *Market Timing for the Nineties*, Stephen Leeb notes that during periods of high inflation, small stocks have returned 21 percent a year, far more than the 16 percent return of gold, the traditional inflation hedge.

Because their performance cycle complements that of large stocks, individually volatile small caps actually reduce the overall volatility of a portfolio to which they are added. Satya Pradhuman, senior quantitative analyst at Merrill Lynch, says that by devoting 10 percent of your equity funds to small stocks, you can boost returns by 40 to 100 *basis points* (hundredths of a percent) without increasing risk *(see the chart at left)*.

Pradhuman warns that if you boost your small-cap allocation above 20 percent, the extra returns come with considerable extra risk. So if you're considering a larger investment in small companies, ask yourself if you can stomach the tailspins along with the vertical climbs.

PBHG fund-family manager Gary Pilgrim advises investors to "be very conservative about money you think you might need over the next few years," using small-fry funds to help put some punch into the rest of your portfolio. Another way to reduce risk is to mix stocks that are insensitive to the economy—among large caps, Campbell Soup Co. is an example—with some that are very sensitive, such as a steel company.

DIVERSIFICATION NEEDN'T STOP at the small-cap level. Small stocks are themselves a disparate lot, and your portfolio should probably contain both growth and value companies and possibly also microcaps and regionals.

Growth versus Value

"Nobody would claim to be a nonvalue investor. It is certainly not the opposite of growth."
— CHARLES ROYCE, *president of Quest Advisory Corp., which manages the Royce family of funds, in an October 1992 interview with* Institutional Investor *magazine*

THE TERMS "GROWTH" AND "value" may apply less to companies and stocks than to two different ways of looking at and evaluating them—that is, to different investment styles. A stock cannot be both small and large (though two investors may place the cutoff at different points); it might, however, be categorized as both growth and value. That's because size is measured along one dimension—market capitalization—whereas growth and value involve two different axes: earnings growth and asset value. A stock's categorization, therefore, depends in part on the perspective from which it is being studied and on the emphasis given different factors. This section defines the growth and value perspectives in general terms.

The growth approach to investing was popularized in 1939 by T. Rowe Price, founder of the eponymous fund company. Price believed that companies, like organisms, pass through three major phases: growth, characterized by increasing earnings; maturity, when earnings stabilize; and decline, when they fall off. The first phase, he felt, offers investors the greatest opportunity for gain with the least risk. Price's followers look for companies with expanding profit margins, quarter-to-quarter sales increases, and a history of accelerating earnings growth, year over year and quarter over quarter. If these criteria are met, growth investors are willing to accept a high share price relative to earnings, a measure known as the *price-earnings ratio,* or *p/e.* Their reasoning is that when earnings have been growing at an ever-faster pace, they should continue to grow strongly enough in the future to narrow the gap with the share price in a short time.

Value investors, in contrast, generally shy away from overblown p/e's. That doesn't mean they discount the importance of earnings, but they are wary of relying on possible future achievements to justify high market valuations in the here and now. Instead, value advocates look at the present (and, to some extent, the past) situation for elements that support a price higher than the current one—for instance, low p/e and low *price-to-book* (the company's market cap divided by its total assets net of liabilities).

"We determine the enterprise's value, [which] may mean looking back a couple of years to when circumstances were better or considering the result of the sale of certain assets or the elimination of losses in certain divisions," Charles Royce explains in the October 1992 *Institutional Investor* interview. "And we try to invest at a discount to that value."

The market should eventually push the stock price up to, or even above, the company's true, intrinsic worth. When this happens, the value investor is gone.

"We like to come in early, when these things are undiscovered or unloved," says Bill Nasgovitz, manager of the small-cap Heartland Value fund. "And when they attract attention or move up in price, we'll gladly part with our stock."

Nasgovitz, Royce, and their fellow value investors are apostles of the almost-legendary Benjamin Graham, whose methods form the basis of the fundamental stock analysis employed today. Since the 1940s, when Graham's ideas started gaining acceptance, and largely because of his teachings, the market has become considerably more efficient, making it nearly impossible to find large stocks that meet his strict criteria. Today's value candidates are found primarily in the small-cap market, which is generally less well followed on Wall Street and is therefore less efficient.

Distressed companies constitute another major group of value candidates, mined mainly by contrarians. Michael Price, a value investor who manages the Mutual Series funds, described the scavenger style in a May 1996 interview with Bloomberg News's Tim Quinson: "Lawsuits, environmental spills, wrong part of the business cycle, companies with disappointing earnings—those are the ponds we fish in."

The rationale is that investors tend to overreact to

ONE STOCK, TWO PERSPECTIVES

IN THE COURSE OF AN ANALYSTS roundtable discussion, I asked growth advocate Jim Oberweis Jr., of the Oberweis funds, and value investor Bill Nasgovitz, of Heartland Advisors, to discuss Just for Feet. The footwear superstore operator appears in both their portfolios, but in opposite positions: Oberweis is long the stock, meaning he actually holds it in his portfolio; Nasgovitz has shorted it—that is, he sold shares borrowed from a broker, planning to replace them with others bought later at a lower price. Why the different approaches?

Jim Oberweis: When we bought Just for Feet, it really was at an attractive valuation. . . . We look for 30 percent growth in revenues. . . . That's actually the bare minimum; in fact, in our portfolio, the average companies grow at a rate of 70 percent. The second thing we look for is 30 percent growth in earnings. Again, an average of about 70 percent in the portfolio.

Chris Graja: So they can't get their earnings by simply laying people off or cutting costs.

JO: Right. These are the most successful, best-managed companies in the business. However, like Bill, we don't want to pay a ridiculous price for the company. I would call us not so much growth investors as growth-value investors. We're looking to buy companies for a p/e not higher than half the rate of growth. So if a company is growing at 50 bad news. David Dreman, a value contrarian and one of the past decade's best fund managers, has stated that while in-favor stocks are notoriously overpriced, out-of-favor ones are just as notoriously underpriced. The trick is to find fallen companies with both low debt and balance sheets strong enough to keep them solvent while good management teams figure out what went wrong and fix it.

Royce, illustrating that the distinction between

---

percent annually, we don't want to pay a p/e higher than about 25. When we bought Just for Feet, I think we paid no higher than $33 ever and an average of about $27. The company is growing at 100 percent annually, in terms of both revenues and earnings. We had outstanding growth in both. And I think that continues. I think it's pretty much a fully valued company at this point. We wouldn't buy it at these levels. But we continue to hold on to it.

CG: Bill, what's the other side of that coin?

Bill Nasgovitz: Well, the flip side would be, we think the stock is fully valued. It is a great company. Great concept. They are a retailer of tennis shoes. No rocket science behind that concept. But at $45 a share, the stock is selling at approximately 60 times this year's estimated earnings. You know, 60 times earnings . . . if you bought the whole company at that price, you'd be getting 1.6 percent on your money. That just doesn't make sense to us.

CG: That's the earnings yield, one over the p/e of 60.

BN: That's the earnings yield. . . . When two-year Treasuries are yielding a lot more: 6.4 percent. So, the stock has had a big move. We think it's a concept that has worked, but margins will be squeezed as the company continues to grow and competitors step into the market. Now, we haven't made any money on the short side yet. It just went into the 50s and we shorted some more. But at this price, we think it's fully priced.

growth and value is one of style rather than substance, finds some of his value prospects among "fast-growth companies ... that have stopped growing as quickly as Wall Street wanted them to. The company may get its act together and be a 20 or 25 percent grower again.... But in the process of that shift, there are a lot of growth investors that become highly agitated." As an example, he cites women's apparel retailer Charming Shoppes, a onetime highflier that he picked up cheap when its earnings flattened. The chain rejoined the fast track after a short breather, and his fund got a nice boost.

BOTH THE GROWTH AND VALUE approaches have advantages. Each also has limitations, which the other side is quick to point out.

Value investors claim their style generates the best long-term results, pointing to evidence like that illustrated in the graphs (right). According to these, a $1 investment in 1975 would have become $52 by 1997 if put in small-cap value stocks, compared with only $29 in small-cap growth, $12.72 in large-cap growth, and $22.79 in large-cap value stocks.

Going further, researchers at Tweedy Browne and investment firm Sanford Bernstein have stated that so-called small-cap outperformance during the past two to three decades is attributable less to size than to deep undervaluation. They point out that, except for three years in which small clearly outshone large, returns for both groups have been almost the same. But when the universe is divided between growth and value stocks, the latter have a significant and consistent advantage.

Moreover, if you adjust returns for risk, small-cap growth comes in dead last among the possible size and style combinations. This is hardly surprising, say value investors, since the growth strategy of buying expensive companies can easily fall flat if future earnings don't increase as fast as expected.

"The way some of these companies are priced, they

VALUE VS. GROWTH PERFORMANCE

SMALL-CAP STOCKS

CUMULATIVE RETURNS OF $1.⁰⁰ INVESTED IN 1976
- Value
- Growth

MID-CAP STOCKS

CUMULATIVE RETURNS OF $1.⁰⁰ INVESTED IN 1976
- Value
- Growth

LARGE-CAP STOCKS

CUMULATIVE RETURNS OF $1.⁰⁰ INVESTED IN 1976
- Value
- Growth

SOURCE: PRUDENTIAL SECURITIES INC.

better become the next Microsoft," Nasgovitz says, "because at 100 or 150 times earnings, one disappointment is going to be extremely painful."

Of course, not every small-cap growth company *is* a potential Microsoft. The chance that a $50 million company will become a $50 billion one is slim. First, the founders need to turn a brilliant idea into a product the whole country knows and uses. Then, when the company really takes off, they need to mutate from hands-on garage inventors to macromanagers. The biggest turning point, though, occurs when the up-and-comer is large enough to attract the attention of the big guys— well-managed competitors with rock-solid balance sheets that can afford to devote some of their resources to putting an upstart out of business.

Growth advocates, for their part, might counter that the statistics showing value's superiority are biased. The studies cited assume a "black-box" style of investing, in which someone blindly buys all the stocks ranked in particular quintiles by their p/e's. This is artificial. Even the most rabid growth investor will avoid the highest ratios. In fact, Claudia Mott, director of small-cap research at Prudential Securities, points out that small-cap growth funds on average outperform small-cap value funds; even Tweedy Browne concedes this in its September 1996 semiannual report.

The growth people also note that though one of their winners could well grow a thousandfold, percent increases for the top value picks are more commonly in the hundreds. Many value stocks, moreover, turn out to be "permacheap," their prices doomed to languish in the low figures. The fact is, most cheap stocks are cheap not because they have been overlooked but because something is gravely wrong with them. And even truly undiscovered stocks may stay underpriced for a long, long time. As Merrill Lynch's Pradhuman puts it, many value investors see value long before anyone else does and, as a result, end up hanging on to stocks through a long unprofitable period.

"When you talk about errors on the value side," says Nasgovitz, "we're generally there a little bit earlier than the rest."

WHERE DOES ALL THIS LEAVE YOU? On the fence, if you're smart. Neither the growth nor the value style of stock picking is infallible, but both are capable of producing winners. And though it's possible for one stock to attract both types of investors, the two groups generally have different takes on a stock and therefore make very different choices. So if you combine both growth and value styles in your portfolio, you'll increase both its diversity and your chances of making successful investments.

Because of their different characteristics, growth and value stocks can perform different roles. The former produce spectacular price rises and just as spectacular falls; the latter, less spectacular but more consistent gains. So growth stocks can provide your portfolio with momentum, while value picks furnish downside protection.

Growth and value also thrive in different market situations. Though value, as I said above, seems to do best over the long term, in certain economic environments growth is dominant. Value, for example, is generally soundly beaten by growth when the economy is slowing, when interest rates are rising, and when the U.S. Treasury yield curve is flat (see the next chapter, Trading Strategies, for details). So my advice here is the same as it was for debt versus equity and large versus small stocks: If you want consistent and reliable returns, make sure both groups are represented in your portfolio. The proportions will depend on your goals and risk tolerance. The chart on the following page shows the risks and returns of different combinations of growth and value stocks, represented respectively by Kemper Growth and Kemper-Dreman Contrarian funds.

If you're in a high-income tax bracket, small-cap growth stocks have a definite edge.

An article in the September 1996 issue of *SmartMoney* points out that if you assume federal and state tax rates of 31 and 6 percent, respectively, small-cap stocks have out-performed large-cap ones during the past 15 years, and growth has beaten out value. Specifically, the average tax-adjusted annual return of the Russell 2000 index of small-cap stocks was 15.1 percent for the period, versus 14.5 for the large-cap S&P 500. During the same period, value stocks in the mostly large- and mid-cap Russell 1000 returned 14.7 percent, versus 14.9 for growth stocks in the same index. The reason for the relative success of the small and growth sectors is that returns of large-cap and value companies derive in great part from the reinvestment of tax-able dividends; in contrast, small-cap and growth compa-nies rely more on capital appreciation, which is taxed at a lower rate than income.

BOTH VALUE AND GROWTH INVESTORS hope their small-cap stocks will get bigger fast, either by matur-ing or by recapturing past glories. Investors in small regional and niche companies generally have more modest aspirations. They're content with solid, steady earnings in relatively noncompetitive environments. Regionals are usually not glamorous, but they may be

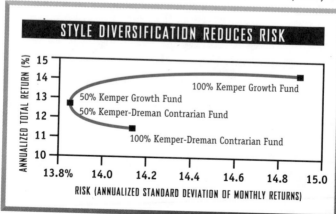

STYLE DIVERSIFICATION REDUCES RISK

100% Kemper Growth Fund
50% Kemper Growth Fund
50% Kemper-Dreman Contrarian Fund
100% Kemper-Dreman Contrarian Fund

ANNUALIZED TOTAL RETURN (%)

RISK (ANNUALIZED STANDARD DEVIATION OF MONTHLY RETURNS)

the friendliest for you, the small investor. They're the ones most likely to be sitting in your hometown, or where your Uncle Bill works. In either case, you're in a position to get some perfectly legal inside information that could give you an edge over the big guys. All you have to do is read the local newspapers, drive by the plant, talk to employees and neighbors, customers, and suppliers.

Small and Smaller

"During the 43 years of our study, $10,000 invested in all the stocks in the Compustat database with a market capitalization below $25 million would have grown to over $29 million! Unfortunately, no professional money manager can realistically **buy** *these stocks."*
— JIM O'SHAUGHNESSY, in *What Works on Wall Street*

REGIONAL, GROWTH, AND VALUE stocks differ in the reasons they're small: because they're parochial, young, or misunderstood. Small stocks can also differ in their degree of smallness. The tiniest of the tiny are the microcaps.

I've defined microcaps as companies having market capitalizations under $250 million. Some in the business put the bar even lower. The Fremont U.S. Micro-Cap fund, for instance, has a median market capitalization of $149.10 million. As I've said before, boundary disputes are common. What isn't disputed, though, is that when you're talking returns, smaller is better. Over the past 20 years, Merrill Lynch's Pradhuman states in a 1995 *Business Week* article, companies with market caps of $60 million or less have produced average annual returns of 21 percent, compared with 17 percent for small-cap stocks and 13 percent for large-caps.

"Historically, this is the group that has given you the biggest bang for the buck," says Prudential's Mott.

Microcaps are even less well followed on Wall Street

than the larger small caps. There are a lot of them, for one thing: Estimates range from 3,000 to more than 4,000. And they cost at least as much to research as larger companies in which institutions can take bigger stakes and make bigger profits. So about 45 percent of the tiniest stocks have no analyst coverage at all, according to Daniel P. Coker, quantitative analyst of the Micro-Cap Research Group at Schroders in New York. Those companies that are covered aren't exactly smothered: Coker figures they average around 1.4 analysts each; the average is less than 1 for caps below $100 million.

That leaves the field pretty much open for you. Uncovering what's going on with an underfollowed company takes a fair amount of time and effort. But think of it as fun, and remember that this is one area where an amateur with a little horse sense and patience can sometimes outsmart an MBA with five investing theories.

"The world has adopted small-cap as a real genre," Quest Advisory's Royce, who specializes in small- and microcap stocks, told *The Washington Post*. "What's remaining [at the lowest levels of capitalization] is below the radar screen, and it's a large area for opportunity."

It's also an area where research really pays off. That's because a small company's performance is determined largely by its own actions and condition, rather than by the economy at large. "As you go down along the scale of size of companies, the success of the company and the investment are much more dependent upon individual company developments," says Robert Kern, portfolio manager of Fremont U.S. Micro-Cap. "I like that the things you are analyzing are closely tied to the company, as opposed to some macroeconomic variable."

Mammoths like AT&T, which spread themselves over many businesses, can't grow much more quickly than the economy itself. Tiny companies, limited to a small slice of one niche, grow principally on the strength of their own products. Of course, if they rely on a few giant customers and these suffer a slowdown, the small suppliers will suffer, too. But really innovative products will always be in demand. Because microcap companies are relatively independent from macroeconomics, good research provides a real edge in this sector: You need a crystal ball to predict where the economy is headed, but a little hard work can uncover customer base and product innovation.

Still, this is a very risky area. The failure rate is much higher for microcap companies than for their larger cousins. Bigger businesses generally have a few past successes to build on, as well as decent managers, capital, and a few long-term contracts to stabilize their earnings. Call it the "survivor effect"—the same inertia that holds giants back in a rising market keeps them afloat in a sinking one. Tiny companies are more agile, but also more vulnerable.

In addition, microcaps are almost invisible and their market consequently illiquid. Want to sell Coca-Cola? Done. Want to sell Lifetime Hoan? Who's the buyer? For microcaps, the average daily trading volume is just 18,000 shares, compared with 54,000 shares for small caps and 505,000 for large stocks, says Pradhuman. Because demand is so low, a seller with an oversupply of micro shares will have to drop his or her price. By the same token, a would-be buyer may have to bid the price way up. This widens *bid-ask spreads*—the difference between where market makers will buy *(the bid)* and sell *(the ask)*. It also amplifies price swings. According to Ibbotson chief economist Paul Kaplan, microcaps are twice as volatile as large-cap stocks and a third jumpier than small ones.

Putting It Together

NOW YOU KNOW YOUR PORTFOLIO should be divided into stocks, bonds, and money markets, and the equity portion between large and small stocks. You might also want to divide your small-cap investments between micro and somewhat larger companies, and among value, growth, and niche stocks. Fine. But how do you go about choosing what exactly to buy in the small-cap categories? The following chapters will provide specific tips. For now, though, here are some general rules and strategies.

Allocate a portion of your small-cap portfolio to mutual funds. Consider making that 100 percent if you don't have enough time to research your picks thoroughly or enough money to spread your risk around. Jim Oberweis Jr. feels that anyone who can't afford to buy 20 individual small-cap stocks should stick with funds. I'd modify that a bit: If you have only $10,000, say, to allocate to this sector, you could invest about $3,000 in one or two well-researched individual stocks and turn over the rest to the professional managers. Investors looking at small caps only for the diversification they provide might do best with an index fund.

Whatever you do with the rest of your small-cap investment money, mutual funds should probably be the vehicle for your microcap investing. A fund gives you diversification, which keeps any one failure from ruining your returns. If you choose well, you also get a skilled manager who has access to the companies' management and the research clout to keep you out of trouble.

Fund management is especially important in the microcap sector, with its relative independence from macroeconomic movements. Since managers can't just ride the trends, their fundamental analysis and business research can make a real difference. As a result, the gap between the best and worst performers in the microcap sector tends to be much greater than in other specializations. In 1995, for instance, Perkins Opportunity, which invests in upstart companies largely from the same upper-Midwest region where the fund is based, returned a stellar 70 percent; at the other extreme, Frontier Equity lost 1.26 percent.

Research, research, research. This advice applies no matter how you decide to invest your small-cap money. You have to do a fair amount of homework to find funds with good track records and, once you've invested, to make sure they hold to their stated objectives. Research is truly crucial, though, when you're looking at individual stocks. As I've said before, the investor with more knowledge always has an edge over the one with less; small caps are one sector where you can glean information not known by the whole world. You also reduce your risks by researching your prospects' finances and weeding out ones that could be toppled by a bad quarter.

Stay small. You don't have the time to analyze all 5,000-plus small companies. For your individual stock investing, you need to reduce your universe to segments where you have an edge and that you can research thoroughly. Many brokerage firms succeed by following companies in one industry or geographic region very closely. Alexander Paris, the president of Barrington Research in Chicago, for example, focuses on companies based in the Midwest. The small-cap mutual funds you buy should probably also be small, limiting the assets they will accept to manage. Remember, this is an area where big guys often have trouble maneuvering.

Keep your costs low. One sure way to lower costs is to minimize your transactions. Trading stock costs you money in commissions and the bid-ask spread.

Small-cap transactions are particularly expensive, since spreads tend to be wide. Most small- and micro-cap stocks are traded over the counter, on the National Association of Securities Dealers Automated Quotations system, or Nasdaq. When you buy or sell shares of these companies, you're dealing not with other investors (as you do on an exchange) but with market makers. These market makers—brokerages, for instance—enter the prices at which they will buy or sell a stock onto an electronic system. The highest buy price and lowest sell price become the bid and offer you see when you get a quote. The difference between the two prices represents the brokerage's compensation for making a market in the stock. The smaller the volume of shares changing hands, the larger the spread.

Despite recent reforms, Nasdaq spreads are often as large as half a point; that means you're buying shares for 50 cents more than you could turn around and sell them for. So if you are to make any money on the trade, the stock's ask must rise more than a half point. On a $10 stock, that represents a 5 percent increase—huge in a market where the average annual return is just 12 percent.

Have a plan for when to buy and when to sell. This is important for funds, but critical for stocks.

Buying is easier. Your goal is to acquire stocks that Wall Street will latch on to a short time later, thus creating demand that will push up their prices. Not every company that produces a fine product and has sound finances fits the bill. Dozens of research studies have shown that stocks go in and out of favor. If you follow your collection of companies carefully and apply a few of the strategies described in the next chapter, you should be in a position to scoop up bargains.

Selling is a tougher call. For now, just remember that you can lessen the pain of your sell decisions by setting both a goal and a cut-loss point for every stock at the time you buy it. If the share price reaches either level, you should reevaluate the company's prospects and its fit with your portfolio to see if there are any new reasons to hold it.

CHAPTER 2

Trading
Strategies

ORE INVESTMENT ideas than money—institutions generally don't have this problem; but many individuals do. So you need to make some hard decisions: Do you spring for the growing company that's capturing the market for satellite-dish beanies? Or do you opt for the fallen angel whose ex-CEO, now in the witness-protection program, has been replaced with Warren Buffett's godson?

This chapter contains suggestions and strategies for making those decisions. Sometimes it's a matter of understanding which broad economic trends may favor one group of companies over another. In other cases, more-localized signals will help you narrow your stock searches or provide a finer mesh for sifting companies to buy from those to watch. None of these strategies is fail-safe. But knowing how to apply them could improve your investing odds. John Spears, a partner at investment advisors Tweedy, Browne Co., contends that even small tilts in your favor make huge differences in the returns of a portfolio held for 20 or 30 years. This book is about giving yourself the edge that will tip the scales.

The Big Picture

"My point of view has tended to be that when small does well versus large, that has mostly to do with what's going on with the U.S. economy. If you go back and look over the course of post-war history, small caps tend to do best when we're coming out of a recession. It tends to be their periods of best return when we are coming out of a very weak economic cycle. I think the problem, though, is that not every recession has led to one of these fabled multiyear small-cap cycles."

— CLAUDIA MOTT, director of small-cap research at Prudential Securities

NATIONAL AND GLOBAL economic trends and events affect which groups and subgroups of investments do better than others. By diversifying your portfolio among the various groups, you achieve stable returns without constantly having to adjust your holdings to the current environment. Still, you shouldn't ignore the larger economic effects discussed in this and the following five sections: the business cycle, both domestic and international; fluctuations in interest rates and in spreads between different credit ratings; foreign exchange movements; and small-cap under- and over-performance. Keeping track of these trends and understanding how they boost or batter which classes of securities will help you make successful investment decisions.

 Vote Democrat.
I don't mean to be partisan, but small-cap stocks do better under Democratic than Republican presidents, according to a Liberty Financial Cos. study reported on in the August 27, 1996, *Investor's Business Daily*. From the beginning of the Hoover administration to the present, the report says, small stocks have risen an average of 22.8 percent annually under Democrats, compared with 1.9 percent under Republicans.

ONE OF THE BIGGEST NATIONAL economic trends is the business cycle. It plays a major role in equity performance: At different points in the cycle, small or large stocks, growth or value, will outperform.

The effect is illustrated in the chart at right, which graphs the relative returns of small growth and value funds against the business cycle, represented by one-year changes in expected earnings per share. When a cycle is just beginning, value stocks tend to do best, according to studies performed by Merrill Lynch senior quantitative analyst Satya Pradhuman. During this phase, earnings (and expectations about them) rise in general, but those of turnaround stocks tend to snap back spectacularly, producing double-digit growth that attracts investors' attention.

Small caps as a group often outperform at the top of the cycle. Large stocks have been played out, and investors must turn to smaller and smaller ones, which haven't been bid up as high, to prolong their roll. The strong bull market of 1995 was a classic case. Big companies had notched up their best showing since 1987, and investors began to look beyond the Microsofts, Intels, and IBMs, which had seen huge gains in the first half of the year, to tinier, less well-known—and cheaper—tech stocks.

People "are always chasing returns," James Floyd, of the Leuthold Group, told *Investor's Business Daily* in August 1995. "And things have turned away from the bigger companies to the smaller ones."

After the cycle's peak, as a slowing economy puts a brake on corporate profits, value stocks fall behind. At this point, says Pradhuman, emerging-growth companies, which still have some earnings momentum, attract investors. During the "soft-landing" period of July 1994 to March 1996, for example, Merrill Lynch's index of small-cap value mutual funds returned just

SOURCE: MERRILL LYNCH QUANTITATIVE ANALYSIS, I/B/E/S, MORNINGSTAR

GROWTH VS. VALUE AS FORECAST EPS CHANGES

SMALL GROWTH/SMALL VALUE FUNDS RELATIVE TOTAL RETURNS

% CHANGE IN EPS

1 Yr Change in EPS *(r. scale)*

Growth/Value *(l. scale)*

1.10 20%
1.05 15
1.00 10
0.95 5
0.90 0
0.85 -5
0.80
0.75 -10

6/83 6/85 6/87 6/89 6/91 6/93 6/95

24.2 percent, compared with 50 percent for small-cap growth funds and 51 percent for the large-cap Standard & Poor's 500 index.

But when recession looms, investors flee small caps altogether for the relative safety and liquidity of large stocks. The best performers in this climate are consumer companies like Philip Morris Cos. and Johnson & Johnson, whose profits are very stable.

"[Small companies] can thrive in a soft-landing environment," John H. Laporte, who manages the $2.1 billion New Horizons Fund, says in a June 1995 *Washington Post* article. "They also can do fine in an environment where corporate earnings flatten out. If, on the other hand, we see a major recession, . . . they will not do well."

In a true bear market, small-cap stocks really suffer. Russell Creighton, senior vice president of Barnett Trust Co., points out in a 1994 *Pensions & Investments* article that when investors can't stand watching their principal erode any further, they start selling their holdings. And this drives down small stocks, which have fewer shares and fewer potential buyers, faster and farther than large ones.

"The liquidity problem is one of the key risks to small stocks," Pradhuman says. "All you need is the same amount of sellers for small as for large stocks, and small stocks go down more because of wider [bid-ask] spreads."

Creighton cautions that a recession now could hit small caps even harder than in the past, because of the growing institutional interest. "Billions of dollars have been put into the markets in the last several years, primarily through mutual funds," he says. "A lot were small cap in the last three years. Mutual fund managers will be forced to sell. We have never had a period with this many small-cap funds trying to liquidate."

On the plus side, the same factors—illiquidity and institutional participation—can drive small stocks to new highs in a generally rising market. Stephen Lieber, chairman of Lieber/Evergreen Asset Management, notes in the *Pensions & Investments's* article that "in a strong market, limited liquidity is an aid. There's less stock around, so if you want it, you have to chase it."

 Don't try to time the market.
After reading about the correlations between the business cycle and stock performance, you might be tempted to try to rebuild your portfolio every time you think you see a new phase starting. Don't do it. First, even the pros can get the signals wrong. Second, the signals point to trends, which are a property of groups and which the individual stocks you hold (or plan to buy) may or may not follow. Third, as Claudia Mott's quote at the beginning of the section points out, even the groups don't always follow the script. And fourth, when they do, the market generally anticipates, rather than follows, economic developments.

"In equity, you're worried about what will happen, not what has happened," says Mark Riepe, vice president of the consulting firm Ibbotson Associates, in an interview in *Pensions & Investments*. "Stocks more often than not are predictors of business cycles." So by the time you see an economic trend forming, it's too late to act on it.

Your best course is to buy the best companies available, then review them when they hit your stop-loss or target price. However, if you're on the fence about a purchase or a sale, the current stage of the business cycle could be a factor that tips you one way or the other.

"We pick stocks because, individually, they are attractive," says Charles Royce, president of Quest Advisory, in a 1992 interview with *Institutional Investor* magazine. "And we can't rely on macro factors to be part of the decision process. Often, too, you get high performance in periods of overvaluation."

My advice for this situation: Handle the business cycle with care. That goes for the other big-picture trends described below, as well. Your best course is to diversify. If she were constructing a portfolio, Claudia Mott says, she would "try to run both disciplines—valuation on the one side, earnings momentum on the other—and structure a portfolio that would look very much like the S&P 600 small-cap index."

A Global Perspective

"More great companies, less coverage."
— Founders Passport Fund manager MICHAEL GERDING'S
Miller Lite theory of international small-cap investing

THE UNITED STATES, OF COURSE, is not the only country with a business cycle. Nor is the U.S. cycle the only one that an investor should consider. Even in our increasingly global economy, nations are rarely in sync—one region's growth will be peaking when another's is just beginning or falling off the edge. The United States, for example, lagged European Community countries in the early '90s only to jump ahead in the middle of the decade.

That doesn't mean you should move your money around the world, chasing the latest hot economy. Rather, you should exploit varying regional cycles as you exploit complementary sector performance: by diversifying.

Small companies are the best medium for global diversification. Most large companies draw at least some of their income from operations abroad. Because of their foreign affairs, they can't be pure domestic plays. On the other hand, large companies' earnings and stock prices are still tied mainly to their home economies, so they don't provide true foreign diversification, either. To get the purest exposure to each country's economic cycle, you have to go down the scale, to small companies that do all their business within their own borders.

Another reason to invest in small foreign companies is that they are where the greatest opportunities are. Two-thirds of the world's market capitalization now lies outside the United States, points out Michael Gerding, manager of the Founders Passport Fund. And, adds Ralph Wanger, the small-cap part of this is generally less efficient. "In many of the emerging markets abroad, it's like the 1960s were here," Leah Zell, the Acorn International fund manager, told *Kiplinger's* magazine in August 1995. "There are fewer analysts, and it's easier to find a good company that's not widely followed."

Put the emphasis on "good." "These aren't bamboo companies in Vietnam," says Gerding. "These are world-class companies, with some of the smartest managers in the world."

The easiest and safest way to internationalize your small-cap holdings is through mutual funds. Foreign markets present challenges that even pros find daunting. Gathering information on the companies is difficult, as is interpreting what you manage to dig up. Paradoxically, investors often have fewer problems in emerging markets, many of which have adopted U.S. accounting standards; some companies in these countries even have Big Six accounting firms for their outside auditors. In contrast, Germany's and Switzerland's accounting rules—particularly those concerning cash reserves and earnings—are very different from their U.S. counterparts. This makes comparing Swiss and German companies' financial statements directly with those of U.S. companies very difficult, if not impossible.

Beyond these obstacles, most governments impose limits and taxes on foreign investors and their profits. You're better off letting a mutual fund manager worry about these headaches, as well as about whether and how to hedge against foreign-exchange risk. Recently, small-cap international funds have been particularly attractive, outperforming those with more general international holdings during the first half of 1996, according to the November 1996 issue of *Bloomberg Personal* magazine.

Interest Rates

"Not surprisingly, when 90-day Treasury-bill rates are overlaid with growth and value cycles, the cycles tend to follow with a reasonable degree of closeness, after a time lag, the longer-term direction of interest rates."

— KENNETH FISHER AND JOSEPH TOMS, president and senior vice president, respectively, of Fisher Investments, in *Small Cap Stocks*

THE ECONOMIC CYCLE is closely allied to the level of interest rates. Money, after all, is the lifeblood of business, and many companies rely on borrowing for their transfusions. When interest rates are low, as they generally are during and just after a slump, companies can fund their projects more cheaply. As a result, their earnings tend to pick up. When rates start to rise again, in response to an expanding economy and fears of inflation, margins erode.

Since earnings drive share price, the equity market mirrors interest-rate levels, rising as they fall, falling as they rise. While he was an analyst at NatWest Securities, Daniel P. Coker did research that confirms this pattern. One focus of his study was stock-market performance during the month following an initial Federal Reserve Board interest-rate change (one reversing the direction of the preceding moves). Coker found that since January 1948, initial rises in the *discount rate* (the rate the Fed charges member banks) were followed by market declines averaging 2.1 percent; initial Fed easings produced average one-month rises of 2.8 percent.

The effect is exaggerated among small-cap stocks. These "are very [influenced] by interest rates in terms of valuations," says Bill Keithler, of the Berger Small

Company Growth Fund, in the 1995 *IBD* article. "When rates are going up, it's very tough sledding." According to the NatWest study, the average one-month declines for large, small, and microcap stocks in response to a Fed tightening were 1.9, 2.5, and 2.6 percent, respectively; the same groups rose 2.2, 4.9, and 6.1 percent after an easing.

The reason for the difference in interest-rate sensitivity is suggested in a 1995 paper by Merrill Lynch's Satya Pradhuman. Although large companies usually borrow in the bond market, he explains, many small companies, because of their lower credit ratings, must borrow from banks at prime. The prime rate is higher than interest rates for investment-grade debt; it also rises faster and falls more slowly. So small-cap earnings tend to respond more dramatically than large-cap earnings to changes in the Treasury rate (the benchmark for corporate bonds).

Kenneth Fisher and Joseph Toms, in the book *Small Cap Stocks*, report similar correlations for value versus growth stocks: "We found that when interest rates drop significantly, with a time lag, a value cycle ensues. Likewise, when rates rise significantly, again with a time lag, the result is a growth cycle."

Why? Because value companies generally carry much more debt, both short- and long-term, than growth companies, which can raise capital more cheaply by issuing stock. Fisher and Toms point out that high p/e ratios, a growth characteristic, translate into cheap capital: Selling stock at 30 times earnings is equivalent to borrowing at a yield of $1/30$, or a 3.3 percent interest rate, which is well below the usual prime rate. In contrast, a p/e of 10, more characteristic of value stocks, translates into a capital cost of 10 percent, and that's seldom better than prime.

So rising interest rates will hit the profits and prices of value companies harder than those of more modestly leveraged growth firms. Conversely, value stocks should shoot up higher under the impetus of falling rates.

Merrill Lynch strategist Steve Kim has found that the slope of the current Treasury yield curve can also be used to forecast whether growth or value will be the better performer. The curve is a graph plotting Treasury yields against various maturities, from three months to 30 years *(see the chart below)*. Its normal shape is gently "positive," with yields rising gradually as maturities increase. This configuration reflects the fact that investors ordinarily require somewhat higher rewards for taking the greater risk of tying up their money for a longer period.

The yield curve may steepen if a Fed lowering of short-term rates, to stimulate economic growth, raises fears of inflation that keep long-term rates from falling proportionately. This signals a good environment for value stocks, which tend to outperform in a hot economy. Conversely, a flatter curve results from a tighter monetary policy, designed to cool the economy, and fewer long-term inflation fears. This configuration is better for growth stocks, which can post decent earnings even when growth is slow.

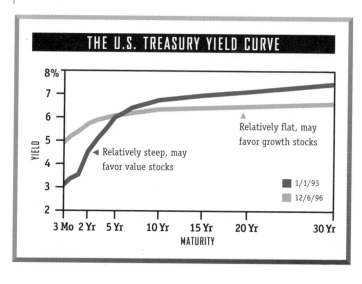

THE U.S. TREASURY YIELD CURVE

YIELD / MATURITY

◄ Relatively steep, may favor value stocks

▲ Relatively flat, may favor growth stocks

■ 1/1/93
▨ 12/6/96

3 Mo 2 Yr 5 Yr 10 Yr 15 Yr 20 Yr 30 Yr

◆ Don't fight the Fed. Rising interest rates mean tough going for stocks, especially small ones. You increase your odds of success tremendously if you take fewer risks and remain hard-nosed about your stock selection criteria when the Fed is tightening.

Credit Spreads

"I'm a bottom-up stock picker. I can't forecast the market or the economy; my shareholders have empirical evidence of this."

— JAMES BARROW, manager of the Vanguard Windsor II mutual fund

THE ABSOLUTE LEVEL OF corporate bond rates is one indicator of what to expect in the small-cap sector. The gap between rates for companies having different credit ratings is another. Both Ibbotson Associates founder Roger Ibbotson and Merrill's Satya Pradhuman have shown that when the spread between the interest rates for lower and higher credit ratings tightens, small caps tend to outperform *(see the chart on the following page).*

One explanation for this relationship is that spreads narrow when the economy is strong, making lenders optimistic about the prospects of risky ventures and willing to give them money at attractive rates. So small companies, which generally fall into the high-risk group, find it easier at these times to get the money they need to feed their rapid growth.

This was certainly true in March and April 1996. From May 1994 to March 1996, investors had required an average of 40 basis points to switch from the security of AAA-rated (bombproof) bonds to shakier BBB-rated (water-repellent) bonds. Then the economic rally began. This panicked traders, who started smelling inflation, and encouraged low-grade-bond investors, who believed it would help riskier businesses. As a result, 10-year bonds backed by the U.S. Treasury lost 9 percent of their value while debt of lesser credits rose a few percent. Meanwhile, funds like Oberweis Micro-Cap and Van Wagoner Emerging Growth jumped almost 50 percent.

Investor's Business Daily carries information about the Treasury curve and credit spreads. This is often provided by Bloomberg News (BN), so the Bloomberg Internet page (www.bloomberg.com) is another good place to look, as are the bond columns in *The New York Times* and *The Wall Street Journal*.
Again, don't use this information to try to time the market. However, if you are deciding between a large stock and an equally attractive small one, a tightening of spreads or a change in the shape of the curve could tip the balance one way or the other. For instance, if you see in *IBD* that the yield difference between AAA- and BBB-rated bonds has narrowed, you might opt for the small company over the large.

The Dollar

"But then one is always excited by descriptions of money changing hands. It's much more fundamental than sex."

— NIGEL DENNIS, English novelist and playwright

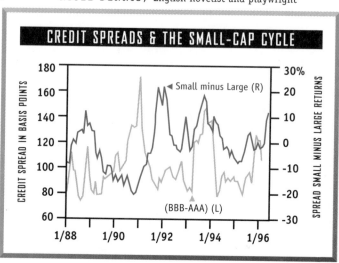

CREDIT SPREADS & THE SMALL-CAP CYCLE

SOURCE: MERRILL LYNCH QUANTIITATIVE ANALYSIS

HERE'S ANOTHER CONNECTION: The dollar exchange rate (how many dollars a unit of another currency will buy) is linked to companies' foreign earnings, which, in turn, are linked to their share prices. When the dollar weakens against foreign currencies, U.S. businesses with overseas sales benefit. Not only are their products now more competitive with foreign-made ones, but their yen or franc earnings translate into many more dollars. Eyeing these profits, investors pour money into the stocks of companies with foreign exposures, most of which are large. A strengthening dollar produces the opposite effect. The overseas profits of large companies are eroded, while homebound small-cap earnings, unaffected by currency fluctuations, draw investor interest *(see the chart on the following page)*.

The first scenario was played out in 1995. From spring to year end, a weak dollar energized the earnings and share prices of large U.S. multinationals such as Coca-Cola Co., Gillette Co., and McDonald's Corp., which draw as much as 40 percent of their revenues from abroad. Meanwhile, small stocks were hit with a double whammy: higher interest rates, which made financing expensive, and a dearth of the overseas business that equity investors were seeking. By mid-1996, though, the second scenario was materializing. Rates had eased, the dollar was strengthening, and profits from multinational operations abroad were becoming slimmer. Analysts saw an opportunity for small, domestic companies to shine.

◆ Finding exchange rates and other currency data is easy—just look in the newspaper. Using this information is more problematic.

All it tells you is which sectors are likely to do better than others. But doing better is not the same as doing well. If you drop only 10 percent while the market drops 20, you've outperformed, but your family still starves. The dollar's relative strength should serve mainly as a warning signal. When it's very weak, as at the end of 1994 and the beginning of 1995, you'd better have rock-solid convictions about any small stock you choose over comparable large ones. A strengthening dollar, on the other hand, lowers the bar.

The Small-Cap Cycle

"People think small caps tend to outperform for seven years and then underperform for some period of time, [but] the relationship really isn't that perfect. ... I think it is very hard to time."
— CLAUDIA MOTT of Prudential Securities

IN ADDITION TO ALTERNATING periods of earnings growth and stagnation, falling and rising rates, wide and tight spreads, and dollar weakness and strength, many analysts detect cycles of small-cap under- and overperformance (see the chart at right). These cycles last from three to more than seven years, depending on who's counting.

The June 1995 *Washington Post* article cited earlier

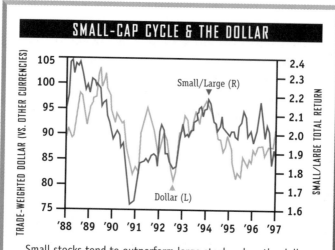

Small stocks tend to outperform large stocks when the dollar appreciates against other currencies.

SOURCE: MERRILL LYNCH QUANTITATIVE ANALYSIS

delineates two recent cycles based on the performance of the T. Rowe Price New Horizons Fund. New Horizons was founded in 1960 as the first small-cap fund and has been used ever since as a barometer for the sector. The *Post* article points out that from June 1983 to October 1990, the fund lost 1 percent while the S&P 500 was gaining 138 percent. That seven-year period was one of the all-time worst for small-cap stocks. The tide turned in October 1990. From that point until March 31, 1995—despite losses during parts of 1992, 1993, and 1994—New Horizons climbed 167 percent, compared with only 88 percent for the S&P 500.

Why do small stocks clobber or get clobbered by large stocks for years at a time? Probably for the same reason that last year's audience favorites will be next year's box-office poison: overexposure. When one group of stocks is in favor, their valuations become extreme. Investors looking for bargains suddenly rediscover last cycle's darlings, which have been snubbed and are now attractively cheap. Money flows into that sector, and the cycle starts all over again.

You can see this process at work by looking at two indicators: first, the relationship between the average p/e of the New Horizons Fund and that of the S&P 500; and, second, small-cap market share.

SMALL-CAP "OVERPERFORMANCE" CYCLES

PERIOD	DURATION (IN YEARS)	CUMULATIVE SMALL-CAP RETURN	ANNUALIZED SMALL-CAP RETURN	EXCESS RETURN VS. S&P 500
1932–37	4.8	946.0	62.5	16.0
1940–45	6.0	534.1	36.0	13.0
1963–68	6.0	267.7	24.2	10.8
1975–83	8.5	1072.6	33.6	14.5
1991–94	3.3	142.8	30.8	11.3
Average	5.7	592.6	37.4	13.3

The theory behind the first indicator is this: Because New Horizons invests in fast-growing small companies, you expect its average p/e to be higher than that of the index, which contains slow growers such as Bethlehem Steel *(see the chart below)*. When the two averages are about equal, therefore, small-cap stocks should be cheap. They may have fallen far out of favor, or the market may not yet have caught on to a recent spurt in income growth. Either way, small stocks are a good buy. This can't last, though—investors will soon rediscover the sector and bid up prices. When New Horizons' average p/e reaches twice the S&P's, small stocks are considered overheated.

The second indicator, small-cap market share, is defined by Fisher and Toms as "the percent of the aggregate value of the total stock market represented by small caps." This number, the authors say, indicates "faddishness."

"When a style has a large share of the market compared to history," they write, "[it] has become more popular. When a style has a low share of the market com-

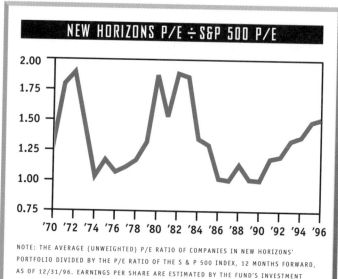

NOTE: THE AVERAGE (UNWEIGHTED) P/E RATIO OF COMPANIES IN NEW HORIZONS' PORTFOLIO DIVIDED BY THE P/E RATIO OF THE S & P 500 INDEX, 12 MONTHS FORWARD, AS OF 12/31/96. EARNINGS PER SHARE ARE ESTIMATED BY THE FUND'S INVESTMENT ADVISOR FROM EACH QUARTER END.

pared to history, it ... has been losing popularity. Generally, styles that are too popular have already been bid up in price—all the buying has been done." They note that small caps went from a market share of only 14 percent in 1974 to a peak of 22 percent in 1983. In hindsight, they say, 1974 was "the best opportunity to own small-cap stocks since the end of the Great Depression."

When the S&P 500 index's average p/e and inflation are both running high, the whole market may be due for a downturn.

According to Gail Dudack, the chief market strategist at UBS Securities, when the Consumer Price Index added to the average p/e of the S&P 500 exceeds 20, trouble is brewing.

The chart below shows that the average p/e of the stock market moves in the opposite direction of the inflation rate. This means that one of the most dangerous times for stocks is when price/earnings ratios are high and inflation starts to rise. That was the situation we experienced in the early 1970s. During the post-World War II, pre-Vietnam war nirvana of the early 1960s, low inflation had supported high stock prices. Then inflation heated up, making life in

INFLATION AND P/E

Average P/E (S&P 500)

Inflation (Year-over-Year Percent Change in CPI)

the '70s and early '80s miserable for investors.

💎 **Watch out when the cash levels of small-cap mutual funds are low—a down cycle in small stocks is about to begin.**

As Prudential's Claudia Mott points out, minimal cash reserves mean the funds are fully invested. So they won't be pouring a lot of new money into small-cap stocks, and growth will probably stall (*see the chart below*).

💎 **Once again, though, don't restructure your portfolio according to where we are in a small-cap cycle. Sure, you'd like to jump in at a bottom and out again at a top. But it isn't that easy.**

The January Effect

"Or is it the January defect?"

— SATYA PRADHUMAN, senior quantitative analyst at Merrill Lynch

THAT DOES IT FOR BIG PICTURE trends. Here's a more modest cycle—one you can pretty much count on year by year. For the past couple of decades, stocks have generated the lion's share of their annual returns in one month: January. The best explanation for this "Jan-

AGGRESSIVE GROWTH MUTUAL FUNDS

Below-average cash levels tend to mean below-average returns.

	SUBSEQUENT RETURN (%)		
CASH LEVEL	3 MONTHS	6 MONTHS	12 MONTHS
<9.7%	2.6	4.6	8.0
Average of 9.7%	2.9	5.8	11.2
>9.7%	3.3	7.0	14.6

NOTE: DATA COVER THE PERIOD JANUARY 1971 THROUGH SEPTEMBER 1995. RETURNS ARE FOR THE NASDAQ COMPOSITE AND DO NOT INCLUDE DIVIDENDS.

SOURCE: INVESTMENT COMPANY INSTITUTE, PRUDENTIAL SECURITIES INC.

uary effect" is taxes. Simply put, at the end of the calendar year, investors sell shares that have fallen in price so they can book losses and reduce their tax bills. Then, after the 30-day waiting period required by law, they buy back the losers they still have faith in. The result is a market decline at year end and a rebound the following January.

This pattern, which has been confirmed by various researchers, is particularly marked among small caps. In fact, a large percentage of the returns that have made the smallest stocks the best long-term performers have come in January. According to Schroders' Coker, since 1926 microcaps have returned 8.7 percent on average during January, compared with 1.4 percent for all months. Merrill Lynch's Pradhuman adds that small value stocks have been the biggest gainers. Connected to this is the fact, also cited by Pradhuman, that the effect has been most pronounced in Januarys following years of poor small-cap performance.

How can you exploit the January effect in your investment strategy?

An easy way to exploit the January effect would be to buy a no-load small-cap mutual fund in December, after it distributes its capital gains, and then sell it again at the end of January. Or you could use fundamental analysis to define a subset of small caps that appear oversold and perform the same trades on them.

If you choose to follow either of these schemes, commit only a small portion of your investment funds, just enough to boost your annual returns. Your general plan should still be to buy excellent companies and hold them for a long time. In this context, the January effect might help you time your trades. For instance, if a small value stock is on your radar near the end of the year, you might wait until prices drop in December to pounce. Conversely, December is probably not a good time to sell shares, unless you want to take a tax loss.

◆ If you like the tax strategy behind the January effect, implement it early.

That's the advice given by Bloomberg applications specialist Sanjiv Gupta in a November 15, 1995, Bloomberg News article. "Smart year-end tax sellers will do it [in November]," he says. "They will get a better price for their shares than they can a month [later]. And—if they are reluctant to part with their losers—they can buy them back at bargain prices in December, when others are dumping them. The wash rule says that when you take a tax loss, you cannot buy the stock [or fund] back for 30 days. Selling early means that you will be in a position to buy them back at the end of December."

To Market, To Market ... IPOs

"When you're working your way toward all-time high levels of IPO activity, it usually means the market's getting a little overvalued. People are obviously trying to take advantage of a very favorable window to get their financing done."
— CLAUDIA MOTT of Prudential Securities

ANOTHER PLACE TO LOOK for smaller-scale signals and trends is the IPO market. An *initial public offering,* or *IPO,* is the first sale of a corporation's stock to the wider community. It's done to raise money and also, sometimes principally, to let existing investors reap big profits on their shares, which will be valued for the first time according to the company's perceived growth prospects. Since IPOs almost always have limited market capitalizations—80 percent are under $60 million, according to Mott—they serve as a litmus test for the small-cap market in general. The volume and quality of deals brought to market in a certain period can signal how hot the small sector is, and how long it's likely to stay that way.

Companies typically do IPOs when they think the

market is riding high enough to bring them a good price for their shares. If many issuers start rushing to market, they may be exploiting a window of opportunity before it closes. In other words, small caps may be due for a correction.

In fact, corrections usually do follow an IPO surge, according to a study performed by Mott. Mott looked at the Nasdaq Composite stock index's performance after months during which a large number of offerings were done. She found that during the past 16 years, IPO activity and small-cap prices have peaked at the same time. In addition, as the chart below shows, returns on the Nasdaq have been flat or negative three, six, and even 12 months after months in which more than 50 IPOs came to market.

Just as important as the volume of IPOs are their price levels—specifically, where the actual prices lie within the "price talk," or presale range set by the offerings' underwriters. A large percentage of deals coming in at the high end of the talk, says Heartland's Bill Nasgovitz, "would indicate [a] tremendous amount of speculation and 'froth' in the marketplace." And

SOURCE: SECURITIES DATA CORP., PRUDENTIAL SECURITIES INC.

AN ACTIVE IPO MARKET IS BAD FOR SMALL CAPS

NUMBER OF IPOs	SUBSEQUENT RETURN (%)		
	3 MONTHS	6 MONTHS	12 MONTHS
<10	11.1	20.4	38.5
11-20	3.4	7.4	11.4
21-30	3.5	5.8	14.3
31-40	2.9	8.0	9.3
41-50	3.7	9.5	16.4
51-60	-0.8	-3.4	-1.2
61-70	-0.4	-1.8	0.0
>71	-1.6	-2.9	-2.7

NOTE: DATA COVER THE PERIOD JANUARY 1979 THROUGH OCTOBER 1995. RETURNS ARE FOR THE NASDAQ COMPOSITE AND DO NOT INCLUDE DIVIDENDS froth signals the end of a rally.

The financial solidity of the companies doing the deals is another factor to watch. "When the portfolio managers I speak to start complaining about the quality of deals," says Mott, "I know we're getting into trouble."

◆ **Your broker can help you find out what's been going on in the IPO market.**
Ask him or her to check the Equity New Issue Calendar on the shop's Bloomberg terminal. This will show the number and total dollar value of deals done every month this year and last. The brokerage should also be able to determine their position within the price talk.

IPOS SERVE AS A SMALL-CAP early-warning system: A lot of activity means that the small-cap market is overheated and you might want to put off purchases until it cools down a bit. (If you discover a really attractive small company selling at what looks like a cheap price, though, don't wait.) Heeding the warning could save you money. But can you use these offerings to make money, as well?

Yes, but not the way you're thinking. You're not likely to rack up big profits by buying IPOs, unless you're a pension fund or some other big shot. My former Bloomberg sidekick Matt Wright, who covered the IPO market for Bloomberg News, says that underwriters allocate all the best deals—the ones that go up 40 or 50 percent the first day of trading—to institutional and large individual investors. These generally make big profits by flipping—buying stakes in the new offerings and then quickly selling them once trading opens.

Investment banks regard IPOs as "the payback to their best institutional or mutual fund clients, like us or Fidelity," John P. Kinnucan, fund manager at the Crabbe Huson Group in Portland, Oregon, told

Bloomberg News in August 1995. "It is a game of mutual back-scratching."

Institutions place orders with a firm's trading desk, paying it tidy commissions, and are rewarded by being let into hot deals at their offering prices. When Netscape came public, for instance, Kinnucan was able to get in early and flip his shares for a profit.

That profit was made possible by us little investors. Like mullets, we listen to the sales hype and place market orders to buy pieces of deals at whatever price is available. As we bid the stock up higher and higher, the institutions unload their stakes. When that drives the price down, we're left holding the bag.

One of the Netscape bag-holders was Blaine Kubesh, who describes himself as just "another sucker." As Kubesh explains it: "I was unfortunate enough to have a pending order to buy Netscape at the market price. By the time I heard it was going to open at over $60, it was too late—I couldn't get my cancel order in quick enough." His order to buy 200 shares was executed at $71. He issued a sell order immediately. It was confirmed at $58.50, landing him a $2,500 loss.

♦ **If you can't beat 'em, join 'em: Invest in a mutual fund that does a good job of flipping.**
According to Morningstar, Garrett Van Wagoner made a king's ransom for his investors by buying and selling IPOs when he was at Govett. To find other champs, read the financial press, which also praises the IPO acumen of the Kaufman fund. Look small, though: The bigger a fund is, the less bang it can get from flipping the relatively small positions they're allotted.

♦ **Be a pilot fish instead of a mullet.**
Other companies in the same industry as a new offering often get caught up in the feeding frenzy surrounding it. So when a hot IPO hits, look for solid stocks in the same sector that you can scoop up at reasonable prices.

Catch 'em later.

Charles Royce, president of Quest Advisory, points out that about a year after their initial offerings, many former high-fliers are lying low: The underwriters have stopped touting them, insiders have cashed in their shares, and many will have had a quarter of weaker earnings. At this point, smart investors can pick up shares of good companies at attractive levels. Waiting also helps you avoid the many one-day wonders. According to Mott, the afterlife of the average IPO is dismal. The most successful—and long-lived—deals have solid fundamentals.

ECONOMIC TRENDS AND CYCLES tell you which sectors and industries should do better than others. To figure out which individual stocks are your best picks, you have to look at the particular, not the general. Cues include company earnings, share-price histories and patterns, and the trades of those in the know. These are the subject of the next six sections.

Beyond Your Wildest Expectations

"Surprise is the great corrector."

— DAVID DREMAN, founder and manager of the Kemper-Dreman funds

EVERYONE LOVES A NICE surprise, and Wall Street is no exception. Investing in companies that report earnings above analysts' expectations produces market-beating returns. That's been the consistent conclusion of research dating back 25 years, and it was recently reiterated in a 1996 report by Mott and Melissa Brown, Prudential's director of quantitative research. The effect of positive surprises, moreover, is enhanced among small companies. These have less analyst coverage and more room to grow, so when one announces better-than-expected earnings, investors listen closely. Mott found that small-cap stocks posting positive surprises generated average three-month returns of 13.7 percent, 10.4 percent better than the S&P 500. By comparison, large-cap surprisers, according to Brown, returned only 5.7 percent on average, or 3.1 percent more than the benchmark.

Mott and Brown also discovered that the positive-surprise effect lasts three months. So you don't have to buy shares the day of an earnings announcement to reap the benefits. That's good news for small investors, who usually get information later than the bigger players and can't act on it as quickly.

You'll find a list of positive surprises at the Primark Investment Research Center Web site (www.pirc.com), published the day after they are announced.

STILL, YOU'D OBVIOUSLY BE ahead of the game if you took your stakes before the stocks were bid up. And you'd really be sitting pretty if you could scoop the market by anticipating positive surprises. But how can you predict when Wall Street's best and brightest will be wrong? Easy. Apply the cockroach theory, which says that when you see one positive earnings surprise, look for others. In 1993 Mott surveyed small companies that had beaten estimates one quarter and calculated they had a 34 percent better chance of doing so again the next quarter than companies that had merely met or fallen below expectations.

Put your stockbroker on the case.
Bloomberg Financial Markets terminal can generate a list of all the companies that produced positive earnings surprises in the current quarter. But bear in mind one drawback to the cockroach approach: Although companies that have previously sprung positive surprises are likely to repeat the performance, they're probably also more expensive than

those that produce surprises out of the blue.

Another, very valuable resource that your broker can put to work for you is I/B/E/S International. I/B/E/S is a subscription-only service that tracks analysts' earnings expectations and publishes a list of the small-cap stocks it feels will beat them. In the past, three-quarters of the firm's picks have turned in positive surprises, and the list as a whole has regularly beaten the S&P 500.

HOWEVER YOU FIND THEM, you should have plenty of surprising stocks to choose from. According to Brown and Mott, nearly 40 percent of companies reporting in the second quarter of 1996 posted earnings that beat estimates, compared with about 22 percent in 1991. Analysts say the increase may indicate that management has discovered the benefits of caution. If a company is too conservative and actual earnings exceed forecasts, the market usually reacts favorably. In contrast, projections that later prove to be overly optimistic can bring lawsuits from disappointed shareholders. So, again quoting Jim Oberweis's September 1996 *Oberweis Report,* managements "tend to work with analysts to keep estimates low."

The result is somewhat like "gradeflation" in academics: Just as grad schools today often give the same weight to an undergraduate's Bs that they used to accord to Cs, so investors increasingly react negatively to companies that merely meet expectations or whose surprises aren't astounding. In October 1996, for example, both Intel and Sun Micro Systems announced third-quarter earnings above their average estimates. The next day Intel was up 5 percent, but Sun was down 9.8 percent. The difference? Unlike Intel, "Sun didn't beat expectations strongly enough," says Furman Selz analyst Martin Pyykkonen, who removed the stock from his "recommended" list. Investor skepticism may perhaps also explain the fact that the duration of the positive-surprise effect has shrunk from six months to three.

When you have a list of companies most likely to fool the wise guys, what do you do with it? You probably don't have enough money to buy shares in them all; even if you did, it wouldn't be a good idea. Remember, you're looking for stocks to hold, not one-quarter wonders, and some surprises could reflect onetime gains, like the sale of property by a company whose real business is computers.

"Understand where the new earnings growth came from, and then question whether it can be duplicated," recommends Christine Baxter of the PBHG family of funds. Did the surprise result from new sales or from onetime non-operational gains? And what effect will the recent outperformance have on future growth? Baxter says that sometimes a young company overworks employees or forces sales on customers before the end of the quarter so that it will meet or exceed its earnings estimate. This can strain resources and put the company in a hole the next quarter, making growth difficult to sustain.

Your best defense against unrepeatable surprises is good fundamental analysis. You can incorporate earnings surprises into the buy-and-hold schema outlined there at either the beginning or the end of the stock-picking process. In the first case, your surprise list will give you ideas to research and analyze; pay special attention to relative strength, since Mott and Coker found that stocks scoring high on this measure were the best performers. In the second case, you'll cull the buy candidates you've already researched for those most likely to surprise analysts with their earnings strength. Either way, if the surprises you expect materialize, you'll be holding solid companies with momentum; if they don't, you're still left with good stocks. I'll take those odds anytime.

This strategy is particularly useful for picking value

stocks. David Dreman, of Dreman Value Management, a manager known for producing high risk-adjusted returns, noted in a 1996 talk at the New York Society of Security Analysts that, though out-of-favor stocks carry less risk than highfliers, they don't add much to your returns if they *stay* out of favor. Earnings surprises, he said, add the juice that boosts value returns above growth.

Dreman cited a study of the period between 1973 and 1993 in which he and Michael Berry (now with Heartland Advisors) looked at how companies' shares performed during both the quarter and the year after they posted positive earnings surprises. All the surprising stocks outperformed, but, as you can see from the chart below, the stars were those with the lowest p/e's: They beat the market by 20 percent during the first quarter following an announcement and by 9.39 percent during the first year. The numbers for the stocks with the highest p/e's during the same periods were 6.63 percent and a mere 0.32 percent, respectively.

If you're worried about the effect of negative surprises on your portfolio, take heart—value will see you through. Dreman and Berry's study also found that one year after missing analysts' estimates, the stocks

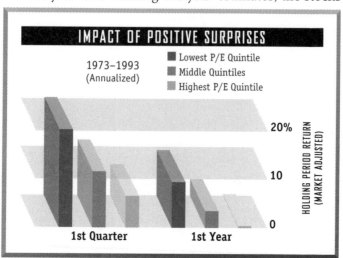

IMPACT OF POSITIVE SURPRISES

1973–1993 (Annualized)

■ Lowest P/E Quintile
■ Middle Quintiles
■ Highest P/E Quintile

20%

10

0

1st Quarter   1st Year

HOLDING PERIOD RETURN (MARKET ADJUSTED)

with the lowest p/e still outperformed. Companies with low p/e's that failed to meet expectations underperformed the market during the first quarter by only about 4 percent, compared with 18.4 percent for high-p/e stocks *(see the chart below)*. And once they pass the one-year mark after a negative surprise, the lowest-p/e stocks generally go on to outperform the market by a slim margin.

♦ Earnings surprises may also indicate the general health of the market.

There hasn't been much research on this. On an anecdotal level, though, Bloomberg markets editor Bill Hester and I have found that in recent history the S&P 500 has posted stunning results when twice as many companies in the index produce positive surprises as produce negative ones. When the two groups run neck and neck, the market has returned a scanty 0.21 percent per quarter. You can find the index's positive/negative ratio on the Bloomberg Internet site (www.bloomberg.com).

Check interest rates, too. Low rates enhance returns in strong earnings quarters and buoy them in weak ones. But beware of quarters where earnings are coming in weak and rates are rising.

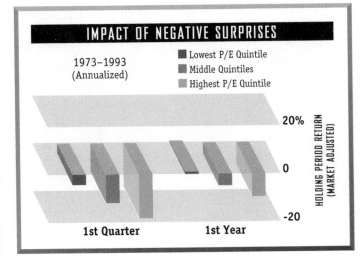

IMPACT OF NEGATIVE SURPRISES

1973–1993
(Annualized)

■ Lowest P/E Quintile
■ Middle Quintiles
■ Highest P/E Quintile

HOLDING PERIOD RETURN
(MARKET ADJUSTED)

20%

0

-20

1st Quarter   1st Year

Estimate Revisions

"It is rare to find a factor that so consistently defines winners and losers."
— CLAUDIA MOTT AND DANIEL P. COKER

ESTIMATE REVISIONS ARE LIKE earnings surprises
with better timing. Say a dip in the cost of raw materi-
als cuts a manufacturer's costs. If the analysts following the company see this and have time to recrunch
their numbers before the earnings announcement,
you've got a revision; if they don't, you've got a surprise.
Either way, the effect is similar—the stock price rises.
It's a matter of math: If a company earning $5 a share
is trading at $50, investors must believe the stock is
worth 10 times earnings; raise the earnings to $10 a
share, and the stock value bounces up to $100.

According to Mott and Coker, buying companies
whose estimates have been revised upward is a great
small-cap strategy. It works for both growth and value
stocks, in up and down markets, and across industries.
Pradhuman agrees. He has found that stocks for which
analysts keep raising their earnings estimates have, on
average, produced annual returns of almost 25 percent.
But be careful. He's also found that they generated
those returns with a volatility of 20.5 percent—that is,
their prices bounced around, with peaks and valleys that
diverged 20.5 percent from the mean. My advice here
is the same as it is for surprises: Use the revisions as a
source for ideas to research or as a final filter for candidates you've already vetted.

You can put together a list of small stocks
whose earnings estimates are being raised by
checking the Bloomberg Internet site (www.-
bloomberg.com).
Or ask your broker; if the brokerage has a lot of clout, like
Merrill Lynch, it should be able to get you the names. And

Zacks Investment Research offers a service on the Internet (www.zacks.com) that will conduct searches like this for $150 a year.

If They Go Up, Buy 'Em!

"The race may not be to the swift nor the victory to the strong, but that's how you bet."
— DAMON RUNYON

MOMENTUM IS A SUPER STRATEGY for a bull market. But at least one Bear has used it, too: Chicago Bear coach Mike Ditka. Ditka made 300-pound William "the Refrigerator" Perry a running back because he figured that bodies in motion tend to stay in motion, and if the body is home-appliance size, watch out! Momentum investors are betting that stocks with a recent history of steadily rising prices are 300-pound backs under a full head of steam.

The investors have a better record than Ditka. Jim O'Shaughnessy, author of *What Works on Wall Street*, has found that since 1954 portfolios composed of the 50 stocks posting the biggest price increases in the previous year have returned about 14.5 percent annually. We've seen the same pattern in the "Bloomberg 100," a list, compiled each January, of the previous year's 100 best performers. The 1994 "100," the first published in *Bloomberg Personal* magazine, went on to trounce the very strong 1995 market.

The companies in that list were almost all small. Merrill's Pradhuman has found that small caps with momentum have returned more than 20 percent a year. There's a catch, though. These stocks have also demonstrated average annual volatility of about 24 percent.

Another caution: Share price may rise for reasons that have little or nothing to do with the quality of the underlying business—the stellar performance of other stocks in the same sector, for example, or rumors that the company is a takeover target. When price increases are not supported by financials, momentum isn't going to carry the stock very far. A refinement of the strategy puts it on a sounder fundamental footing by shifting the focus from price to earnings.

The father of earnings-momentum investing is Richard Driehaus, a Chicago broker who manages over $1 billion in assets. His reasoning is that since earnings drive stock prices, companies with accelerating earnings should outperform. American Century Investors fund managers, who use this approach, explain in a February 1996 *Kiplinger's* article that they apply Driehaus's insight by looking for companies whose profits and revenues are growing at least 30 percent, year over year and quarter over quarter. They then narrow their choices by talking to analysts and managements to determine if the companies' acceleration will continue. For instance, the funds pounced on computer chipmaker Burr-Brown after learning that the company was selling its new higher-margin analog chips as fast as it could produce them. American Century started acquiring the stock at 25 to 30 percent above the previous day's close and kept right on buying.

Gary Pilgrim also looks for accelerating earnings growth—of at least 20 percent—but he requires upward estimate revisions and positive surprises, as well. According to Morningstar, his PBHG Growth ranks among the top five of all funds in 5- and 10-year performance. Pilgrim told *Kiplinger's* in an October 1996 article that he uses a combination of revisions, surprises, and growth, weighted 35, 25, and 40 percent, respectively, to rank the stocks in the PBHG universe: 10 is perfect; 1 means forget it.

In contrast to the American Century managers, Pilgrim prefers not to know too much about the operations of the companies he owns. Instead, he uses statistical measures to calculate each one's underlying long-term growth rate. "My objective is to know how these companies are doing, as opposed to what they are doing," he told *Kiplinger's*. "It's much more important to know that analysts are raising earnings estimates, that competitors aren't gaining ground, that controversies over products are being resolved. In other words, I want my knowledge to be a mile wide and an inch deep."

Both American Century and PBHG agree, though, on pulling the plug when the acceleration that attracted their attention begins to slow. First Team Sports, a maker of in-line roller skates, for example, dropped out of the American Century universe when its annual revenue growth fell from 100 percent to 48 percent and management began painting a less rosy picture of its prospects.

♦ **Check historical earnings rates in the S&P 600 guide or the company financial reports.**
Again, use this research either to suggest ideas or to screen your finalists. But remember, one of the momentum managers' most important assets is discipline—they adhere strictly to their criteria for buying and, in particular, selling.

THE EARNINGS MOMENTUM STRATEGY can pay off big: American Century Vista and PBHG Growth returned 47 and 50 percent, respectively, in 1995. But, like price momentum, it can also bomb. Vista and PBHG dropped about 41 and 50 percent at one point in 1987, and 15 and 9 percent in 1990. If you can't stomach this much volatility, try the Aurora approach.

Aurora

"If you want a Ferrari, you gotta pay for a Ferrari."
— GARRETT VAN WAGONER

THE MAIN REASON THE RETURNS of strict momentum investors like Gary Pilgrim and the American Century managers vary so widely is that their models have no value component. "If we can find securities that have a year or two of positive surprises ahead of them, the p/e today doesn't matter," Glen Fogel, manager of the American Century Giftrust fund, told *Kiplinger's*, "because growth overwhelms the current valuation."

That may be true, and Giftrust did return 38.32 percent in 1995. But value criteria can provide a useful safety valve. By looking at p/e and price/book ratios, momentum managers might avoid buying grossly overvalued stocks. Value criteria might also help them discern when a theme has run its course and it's time to jump ship.

Adding a value safety valve is fairly easy. It's also profitable. O'Shaughnessy found that when he pared his list of stocks with good price momentum to just those with price-sales ratios less than 1, average annual returns since 1954 increased to more than 18 percent. You can put O'Shaughnessy's research to work for you by applying it to the "Bloomberg 100," selecting the companies with price-sales ratios less than one.

Aurora is another, more mathematically rigorous approach to tempering a fundamentally emerging-growth style with value. Its designer, Merrill's Satya Pradhuman, uses a model that ranks stocks—from a low of 1 to a high of 100—according to a weighted combination of three factors: the first is relative strength, which is measured by a stock's percentage price increase over the past year. The second is the size of positive earnings-estimate revisions. And the third is a "valuation" component emphasizing low price to cash flow (a measure similar to p/e but less vulnerable to accounting manipulations) relative to the stock's industry sectors.

The Aurora portfolio is composed of the stocks scoring in the top percentile when the strength, earnings, and valuation components are assigned weights of 40, 30, and 30 percent, respectively. From February 1980 through December 1995, this approach returned a whopping 31 percent a year, with 225 basis points less volatility than pure momentum.

In a less bullish market, Pradhuman thought it would be wise to change emphasis, to a basic value style spiced with growth. So he also created the Enhanced Contrarian Portfolio, using fundamentally the same model but changing the weightings to 70 percent value, 15 percent strength, and 15 percent earnings. This approach generated returns of almost 25 percent per year from 1980 to 1995, with volatility of 20.5 percent.

The Aurora and Contrarian portfolios share an Achilles heel, though: If the market really tanks—dropping, say, 8 percent in a month—both will get spanked, perhaps even slightly worse than stocks picked using other methods.

You can create a poor man's version of Pradhuman's portfolios using the Friday edition of Investor's Business Daily, which lists stocks' percentile scores for relative strength and earnings momentum.
Pick out the ones with the highest scores and lowest p/e's, and research them. Then apply one of Pradhuman's weighting systems. Finally, choose the high scorers with the best fundamentals.

Insider Trading, the Legal Way

"Executives have a good insight into an industry, where Wall Street sometimes has a myopic view."
— THOMAS FITZGERALD, president of T.H. Fitzgerald & Co., which runs the Reserve Informed Investors Growth Fund

INSIDERS—OFFICERS, MEMBERS of the board—should have a better idea of a company's prospects than any outsider, no matter how talented. They have what Tweedy, Browne Co., in its customer booklet, terms "insight information": firsthand knowledge of new marketing programs, planned cost efficiencies, and price hikes, as well as industry conditions. You can trade on this information indirectly by watching when insiders buy company stock. This tells you that the people who really know the business have enough confidence in its future to stake their own money on it.

"We like to invest alongside the people that run the companies," says Praveen Gottipalli, a principal at Symphony Asset Management, which manages Bear, Stearns & Co.'s Insiders Select Fund.

Buying with the insiders certainly worked for purchasers of Guidant Corp. shares. In late September 1995, roughly a year after it was spun off by Eli Lilly & Co. at 14^1/$_2$, the medical-device maker's chairman, president, and chief financial officer all bought large blocks of its stock. The share price at the time was 26; a year later it had more than doubled, to 55^1/$_2$.

Nejat Seyhun, a professor of finance at the University of Michigan, conducted a study of the one-year performance of companies following a year in which insiders were either net buyers or net sellers of their stock. Seyhun found that companies associated with insider buying beat the market by almost 5 percent, while those associated with insider selling performed worse than the market.

When sorting through your investment ideas, check your prospects' insider-trading histories. Anyone who owns more than 5 percent of a company's shares or holds a high position in its management must notify the Securities and Exchange Commission whenever he or she trades the stock. You can find out who's done what by checking form 4 (which must be filed by any insider trading a company's shares) and form 144 (filed by holders of restricted stock); both can be accessed on Edgar—short for Electronic Data Gathering Analysis and Retrieval—which you can access at www.sec.gov/edgarhp.htm.

If purchases accounted for the greatest dollar volume of insider trades during the past year, that's definitely a plus. Selling is a much less perfect indicator: Though people generally buy stock for only one reason—because they think it'll make them money—any number of reasons exist for selling, and some have nothing to do with the company's prospects. An executive may want to diversify his portfolio, for example, or need the cash to pay his daughter's college tuition. Also bear in mind that the absolute number of shares someone sells is less important than the percentage of his or her total stake this number represents. For example, the fact that Microsoft chairman Bill Gates sold 520,955 of his company's shares in August 1996 looks less significant when you realize that he still holds 141 million.

Once you've made your purchases, keep an eye on insider activity. It could tip the balance if you're wavering between holding and selling a stock.

A VARIATION ON INSIDER PURCHASING occurs when the company buys back its own shares on the open market. This is a good sign for several reasons. By reducing the number of shares outstanding, a buyback raises earnings per share and reduces the amount of money that must be paid out in dividends. Perhaps most important, though, it usually indicates that company officers feel the stock is cheap. So if you follow management's lead, you could be picking up a bargain.

Share price does tend to increase after a buyback. According to a 1994 study by Rice University professor David Ikenberry, stocks rise an average of 3 percent the day an announcement is made and then beat the market by 12 percent over the next four years.

With results like that, buybacks should definitely have a role in your stock selection, either as a source of ideas or as a screen. They're a particularly good signal when you're choosing value investments. In the Rice study, buyback stocks that were cheap according to value criteria "returned an average of 45 percent more over a four-year period than similar nonbuyback stocks."

Be a little skeptical, though. Ask yourself why a company is spending its money on its stock rather than on its business. Has it run out of growth opportunities and products to research? Or is the buyback just a quick way to boost share price? Often the announcement itself accomplishes that goal, and the companies never actually follow through. In fact, some analysts estimate that only a third of the shares slated for buybacks get repurchased. Empty talk won't sustain share price long.

If you buy a stock on the basis of an announced buyback, check the next quarterly statement to see if shares outstanding have decreased, indicating that the company is making good on its promise.

Another way to profit from other people's purchases is to jump into stocks just before the big guns discover them.

Many professional investors will look for stocks with very low institutional ownership and hope that new-product launches or earnings surprises will draw fund managers' attention. A tiny stake by institutional standards can be enough to drive a small company's shares sky-high.

You'll find the percentage of institutional ownership among the Key Stock Statistics in the S&P guide reports. If the company isn't in the guide, ask your broker to check Morningstar, Bloomberg, or the charts put out by *IBD* publisher O'Neil & Co. Make a low institutional stake one of your sorting criteria, but not a must-have.

Technical Marks

"I use fundamentals and technicals closely. Fundamentals are first, and if you have them, you have a huge advantage. But market conditions change, and you need to have a plan for that. I often use fundamental analysis to determine how much downside a stock might have. The ideal situation is when our fundamental upside is three or more times greater than [the stock's technical support level]—for example, where we see the upside as being 50 percent, but the downside is only 10 percent."

— LISA GRAY of PaineWebber

PRETTY MUCH ALL THE STRATEGIES discussed to this point have involved fundamentals, such as the figures on a company's balance sheet and income statement. The reason is that they give you a window on how a business is run and what management thinks. Many analysts ignore them, though, and focus not on a company's business but on the stock itself. Technical analysis, as this approach is called, treats a company's shares as commodities subject to market forces that can be traced by charting trade-volume and price trends. Analysts use the patterns revealed in these charts to predict where a stock is headed.

If you want to find out how they do that, read Thomas Dorsey's book, *Point & Figure Charting*. Listening to some tech guys, you'd think the waves and angles they graph were cabalistic symbols with mystic connections to the future. Dorsey brings it all down to earth, invoking the prosaic forces of supply and demand. The idea is to deduce from the patterns of volume and price moves whether sellers or buyers are dominating the market. You want to be holding a stock when buyers outnumber sellers.

To determine who has the upper hand, techies may use bar and line graphs, which plot share price and trade volume against time, or point-and-figure charts. Dorsey favors the latter. These indicate the magnitude and direction of share-price moves, but not the time they occur: Each square represents a specified price unit; when a stock's price moves up a unit, an X is put in the square above the previous point; when it falls, an O is entered one square down. Whenever the direction changes, the marks are made one column over, so each column contains either all Xs or all Os. An example of a point-and-figure chart, for Veterinary Center of America, appears at right.

Charting—whether by bar, line, or point and figure—reveals patterns, which must be interpreted. Interpretation involves a combination of science and art. Some of the signals are pretty clear. When each rising trend reaches a summit higher than the previous one, the buyers (bulls) are riding high; seller (bear) domination is indicated by successively lower falls. When both rises and falls remain within a narrow horizontal band, the stock is said to have stabilized, or based; if this period of stasis was preceded by a rise, it will probably be followed by a further rise; a preceding drop foreshadows a future fall.

Often a chart will show a series of peaks or dips that reach but never pass a particular price. The ceiling to rises is termed a resistance level; the floor to drops, a support level. Similar to these are trend lines, which connect series of declining peaks or rising dips. When a stock's price breaks through a resistance level, it means that investors are willing to buy at higher levels than in the past; a fall through a support level signals willingness to sell at lower prices. Breaching a trend line may presage a change in the direction of price movements.

Opinions are divided on how great a role technical analysis should play in small-cap investing. Charts are

EXAMPLE OF POINT AND FIGURE CHARTING

Veterinary Center of America (VCAI)
(5/16/94 - 1/8/97)

most valuable, technicians say, in liquid markets, where information is freely available and which are too large to manipulate. For example, in the huge government bond market, crucial information, such as employment, GDP, and inflation figures, is kept quiet until it can be released to all players simultaneously. So T-bond price and volume movements are good indicators of where other players in the market are willing to buy and sell. In the small-cap sector, in contrast, the prices of the many thinly traded, low-priced stocks are easily manipulated. An unscrupulous investor with a lot of microcap shares to unload might pick up a large block of the stock at a higher price, hoping others would notice the volume and assume the smart money was loading up. With duped investors rushing to buy the stock, the manipulator would be able to sell his stake at a tidy profit.

Ease of manipulation reduces the reliability of small-cap price and volume patterns. Accordingly, many investors in the sector use technical analysis merely to supplement their basic fundamental analysis. Dorsey, for example, infers from his charts how defensive or aggressive an investor should be. Other managers employ technicals to reduce their risk—to ensure, say, that an undervalued company isn't going to stay that way too long. Bill Nasgovitz is one of those. Though charts aren't a cornerstone of Heartland's stock-picking strategy, Nasgovitz does what technical types call base building. He looks for out-of-favor stocks whose charts resemble "a dead man's heartbeat"—in other words, flat-liners whose prices have based after a period of decline and, he hopes, are poised to take off.

Nasgovitz wants to be the first to discover a story. Jim Oberweis, in contrast, feels that other investors are too smart to get scooped too often. He becomes concerned if nobody else is excited about one of his picks. So he looks at charts like those published by O'Neil & Co., which plot relative strength, for signs of an uptrend and market outperformance.

◆ Keep technicals in perspective.
Over the long run, fundamentals drive stock prices, period. But if you can check a chart, do it: You'll reduce your risk by looking for good value and growth companies that are emerging from a base.

◆ Some of Tom Dorsey's research appears on the Internet at www.dorseywright.com. Try e-mailing that address for help finding a local brokerage with good research on small stocks that could also chart your holdings.

UP TO NOW, I'VE TALKED ABOUT using economic, fundamental, and technical signals to decide what stocks to buy and sell when. The remaining sections discuss more esoteric trading techniques and instruments, as well as cost-cutters.

Going Short

"We've put together a relatively small short portfolio of about 15 of Wall Street's most overvalued, most overloved securities, which we think are ripe for a fall."
— Heartland funds' BILL NASGOVITZ

RULE NUMBER ONE IN SMALL-CAP investing: Beware of froth. When companies become Wall Street sweethearts and institutions own a large percentage of their shares, not enough demand remains in the market to drive their prices higher. Worse, their high p/e's increase the risk that one disappointment will send them tumbling.

Such stocks are poor buys. But they're good candidates for *shorting*—selling shares borrowed from a broker in hopes of replacing them with others bought later at a lower price. Bill Nasgovitz uses this tactic for his Small Cap Contrarian fund, which can have as much as 25 percent of its portfolio in short positions. Nasgovitz improves his odds by looking for frothy stocks that are being sold by company insiders *(see above)*.

"When we're buying shares, we like to see insiders expressing their confidence by buying, too," he says. "With shorts, it's just the opposite—we look for high-flying stocks where there's been strong and consistent insider selling, in size."

Nasgovitz probably also limits his shorting to the larger companies within the small-cap sector. The smallest stocks are thinly traded, making it too easy for shorts to get caught in a squeeze—forced to buy scarce shares at high prices to replace the borrowed ones they sold.

Short selling is not for the general public. You need time and patience and—most of all, warns Nasgovitz— a good stomach. "You sell something at 20, it might go to 30 in this market," he says. "It's difficult to do, to handle your emotions."

Here's a less stomach-churning way, also used by Heartland, to make money on short sales. Start with your group of thoroughly researched, solid companies, and buy those with high short interest—your broker can check the stock screens for you, or you can look yourself at the back of *Barron's*.

The key to this strategy is that all the shorts will ultimately need to buy shares to cover their positions. Of course, they could know some deep, dark secret about a company that will keep its price in the dumps despite their purchases. So check what insiders are doing. If the corporate execs, who really know the company, are buying, you can be more confident that the shorts are wrong and that their covering will drive the share price up.

PAIRED TRADING

"[Trading stocks in pairs] is a way to contain risk but still play with some of the juicier, riskier types of securities."

— ERIC KOBREN, money manager and the publisher of *FundsNet Insight,* in an interview with Scott Schnipper of Bloomberg News ·

A VARIATION ON SHORT SELLING that Nasgovitz likes to use in his Contra fund is paired trading. It's like betting the spread in football: What counts is not who beats who, but by how much. A paired trade is a bet that the best company in an industry will thump the worst. The bigger the spread, the more you earn.

It works like this: You take a long position on your pick to win while shorting your designated loser. Then if the two companies perform as you expect, you pocket profits from both ends.

Paired trading also provides protection against bad bounces. Say you hold complementary positions in an industry that tanks, as the semiconductor group did in fall 1995. Your profits from the shorted stock will offset your losses on your long bet.

In spring 1996 Nasgovitz pulled off a successful paired trade in the videoconferencing industry. The laggard of the group, Boca Research, was an ideal value buy. Despite the fact that its earnings had soared 50 percent the previous year and it had recently announced plans to bring videoconferencing to personal computers, the company was trading at only about 13 times estimated earnings. In contrast, Picturetel Corp., whose book value of $6.09 a share was comparable to Boca's $6.50, was selling at 37 times earnings, topping the sector.

Nasgovitz bought the first and shorted the second in early spring. By April, Boca had moved little, but Picturetel shares had tumbled to 29¾ from a February peak of almost 45, allowing Contra to cover its position and realize a profit.

Paired trading works best when equities are neither roaring ahead nor going down the chute. A rising market can buoy even the fumblers, and a falling one can sink the best-run companies; either way, there won't be many stocks headed in radically different directions to create the yawning spreads you need to exploit. A stagnant market is also exactly the environment in which you need ingenious ploys like this to spice up bland returns.

In any environment, however, this technique, like straight shorting, is probably best left to the pros. Even they make miscalls. Dallas-based money manager David Tice, for instance, paired Sullivan Dental Products and Patterson Dental, two comparable companies whose market valuations seemed out of line with their fundamentals: Sullivan's too low, at 1.6 times book value, and Patterson's too high, at almost 6 times book. Tice bought the first and shorted the second. Patterson proceeded to rise almost 5 percent, while Sullivan advanced a mere 1 percent.

If you decide to try this at home, start by sorting through your list of researched candidates for the best value prospect. Then enlist your broker's help to find its evil twin—a company in the same business whose fundamentals don't seem to support its share price.

Next check insider activity. You want to see the companies' officers on your side of the trades, buying your long pick and selling your short. Finally, to be certain you're not walking into a squeeze, have your broker pull up your short candidate's *short-interest ratio*. This tells you what percentage of the stock's daily trade volume the total outstanding short positions in it represent. If the percentage is too high, you'll have a lot of competition when you go to cover, which will drive up the price .

CALL OPTIONS AND CONVERTIBLE BONDS

"Be careful with derivatives. Bad judgment and borrowed money can be a dangerous combination."
— WARREN BUFFETT

ANOTHER WAY TO CASH IN on a small company's growth is to invest in its stock without buying any shares. Sounds like a pretty good trick, huh? Actually, it's just derivative business as usual. By purchasing equity call options or convertible bonds instead of the stock itself, you can benefit from a short-term rise in share price with less exposure to a fall.

An *equity call option* is a contract conferring the right (but not the obligation) to buy 100 shares of a company's stock at a specified price, called the *strike price,* on or before a specified expiration date. The option's price, or *premium,* is determined by two factors: its *intrinsic* and *time values.* A call option's intrinsic value is the difference between its strike and the stock's current share price, as long as the latter is higher. If the share price is lower than the strike, the option has no intrinsic value. It still has time value, though, which reflects the market's estimation of the likelihood that the stock price will reach or surpass the strike before the option expires.

For instance, at the end of July 1996, when Intel was selling at 74, or $7,400 for 100 shares, you could have picked up a call option on its stock, expiring January 1999 and with a strike of 100, for $1,000. Since the strike was higher than the current share price, the premium was composed entirely of time value. Say that eight months later Intel stock rose to 146. Your option would then have had an intrinsic value of $46, and its premium would have risen accordingly. You could sell it at this point and realize approximately the same capital gain as if you had bought and sold 100 shares of the stock.

Of course, if the share price fails to rise above the strike before the expiration date, you lose the entire premium. This sum, however, is considerably less than the cost of the 100 shares the option represents—in the example, $1,000 versus $7,400. So a call option effectively gives you the same profit opportunity as 100 shares of stock (though you miss out on any dividends) while putting much less of your principal at risk.

On the other hand, stock ownership has an important advantage over option investing: A stock, unlike an option, always has time value. Most options have lives of less than a year. *(LEAPS, or long-term equity anticipation securities, are options with longer maturities—two to three years—and much higher price tags.)* If you own a three-month call and the underlying shares shoot up from nowhere after three months and one day, you're out of luck. If you own the stock, though, you can wait the extra day—or an extra month, or a year—and still profit.

For that reason, options are not good for investing in value stocks, which can languish at low price levels for long periods. Because of the downside protection they afford, they're probably best for investing in the smallest, and most volatile, companies. Few of those, however, issue options. To follow the derivative route here, you'd have to switch markets and look into convertible debt.

A *convertible* is a corporate bond that can be exchanged for shares of the issuing company's stock. Each bond is associated not only with a yield but also with a conversion ratio, which specifies the number of shares per $1,000 of face value the investor is entitled to. For instance, if you bought a $10,000 Pee Wee Corp. convertible bond with a ratio of 250, you could exchange it for 2,500 shares of Pee Wee stock. Because the conversion feature acts like an equity call option, the market value of the bond rises with that of the stock. It will also fall as the share price falls, but usually not as far. The bond is cushioned by its own investment value (the price at which an identical bond without a conversion feature would trade) and the time value of the option component.

"It's like buying the stock and getting a 7 percent yield while you wait for it to take off," says Eric Miller, an analyst with the Heartland Value Plus Fund, which has about 17 percent of its assets in these bonds.

Convertibles are well suited to value investors like Heartland. The issuers are generally small or obscure companies, which would find straight debt structures prohibitively expensive. The bonds also tend to be thinly traded. All this makes for just the sort of market on which value investors thrive.

"When you consider that the stock is underfollowed and then include the fact that many of these bonds aren't rated and many institutions are excluded from buying them, you have an extra degree of inefficiency," says Miller, who has exploited this inefficiency quite successfully. The Quantum Health Resources convertibles that he bought at 76.90, for instance, surged soon afterward to more than 92, an increase of almost 20 percent.

The same characteristics that make convertibles attractive value plays also make them risky for individual investors.
Because they're often not rated by S&P or Moody's Investors Service, you have to do a lot of digging yourself to find out how likely the issuing companies are to default. The odds of failure may well be higher than you find comfortable. So be careful: Don't buy the convertibles of any company whose stock you wouldn't invest in.

A PENNY SAVED

NO MATTER HOW GOOD your stock picks are and how disciplined you are about selling, you'll always do better if you can keep your transaction costs down. Here are some other, more sophisticated, tricks of the trade:

◆ **When you buy a stock, place a limit order between its bid and ask.** Occasionally your order will fill and you'll end up with a price that's better than the one market makers are offering.

◆ **Ask your broker to put your order on Instinet or Bloomberg Tradebook.** These are fast-growing systems used by a number of OTC departments to place offers within the spread for dealers to see and act upon. They are fairly recent innovations; ask if your broker has access to them.

◆ **See if your broker will allow you to match trades within the brokerage or its market maker.** Charles Schwab Co., through its Assurance Trading program, is one of the few firms that offer this service. If you're allowed to do it, matching can get you a better price than the bid or ask. It may not work too well, though, with small stocks that don't trade heavily, because there won't be many people willing to take the other side.

Small-Cap
RECAP

THIS IS THE END. Now I've given you every technique and tactic I know for making money in small stocks. The danger is that in all the details, you can lose sight of the fundamental investing process. So here, in summary, are the basic precepts.

Be an investor, not a speculator. This book is about achieving superior returns over a long term with reasonable risk. Small-cap stocks play an integral role in that process, but only as part of a balanced portfolio whose makeup reflects your long- and short-term savings goals.

So, diversify. Invest in both small and large stocks—in domestic and foreign companies— that reflect both growth and value styles. Put enough money in cash and bonds to take care of expenses looming in the near future. Then, with the rest, you can ride the equity market's ups and downs, ultimately reaping its superior long-term returns.

Look for great companies at good prices and good companies at great prices. As Warren Buffett says, growth and value are joined at the hip. A crummy business that can't make money is no bargain, no matter how cheap it is. Even a wonderful business won't make you much money if its market value is hyperinflated.

Exploit your edge. The markets, by and large, are very efficient. Few good companies stay undervalued for long. The guys who make real money are the ones who find out first about whatever it is that drives a stock's price up. Your chances of scooping Wall Street on one of the big companies are almost nil. The odds get better as you go down the scale in size. With small companies, which are not well followed on the Street, special knowledge of a business or acquaintance with management can give you a real edge to exploit.

Tip the odds in your favor. You're searching for companies with great products, whose management you trust and whose financial house is in order. But not every good business is a good buy—you need some indication that the share price is going to increase. Success is more likely if the stock meets the following criteria:

1. earnings yield is higher than corporate bond yields.
2. Its price-to-sales ratio is less than 1.
3. It is priced below book value.
4. Its ROE is greater than 20.
5. It is being bought by insiders or by the company itself.
6. Analysts are raising the company's earnings estimates.
7. Earnings consistently exceed expectations.
8. Sales and earnings are growing faster than 30 percent annually, or quarter over quarter, or both.
9. The company has a strong brand name or dominates an industry or niche.
10. The stock has been outperforming the S&P 600.

Buy to hold. Invest only in companies you feel comfortable living with for a long time. Jumping in and out of stocks costs too much in fees, spreads, and taxes to be profitable, even assuming you could time your trades successfully.

But don't be sentimental about your investments. You'd better have a good reason for holding a stock in the following situations:

1 The company's p/e is greater than 1.5 times a conservative estimate of its long-term earnings growth rate.
2 Insider selling of its shares exceeds insider buying.
3 The company carries more debt than equity.
4 Its management or investor relations officer sidesteps your questions.
5 Growth in earnings, revenues, or profit margins has declined in several consecutive quarters.
6 The company posts earnings significantly below analyst expectations.
7 Analysts lower their earnings estimates.
8 Analysts rate the stock a sell.
9 The stock has consistently underperformed the S&P 600, and management has not enunciated a clear plan for turning things around.
10 Everyone loves it.

Enjoy yourself. Some people get a kick out of doing research and playing with numbers; others leave that to the pros by investing in well-managed mutual funds. Whatever your style, you should get a warm feeling watching your savings grow.

Resources

HERE ARE SOME sources you can use to delve more deeply into the topics touched on in the book, as well as to implement the strategies discussed. They're divided into three sections: **READING MATTER**, which lists the books, newsletters, and magazines mentioned in the text, together with some additional ones you might find helpful; **WEB SITES**, containing useful Internet addresses; and **REGIONAL BROKERS**, which provides the names and phone numbers of some brokerages that specialize in companies located in particular areas of the country.

Reading Matter

ENTRIES PROVIDE PUBLISHING or subscription information, but before you shell out a lot of money, you may want to check your local library's holdings.

Books

BOOKS ARE SOME OF THE GREATEST tools for an investor. By spending about 10 to 50 bucks and a few days studying, you can absorb knowledge that it has taken some smart person years to acquire. Though I mostly advocate bottom-up, buy-and-hold investing, I've included in the list below books on other disciplines and trading, which will give you a broader understanding of how the stock market really works.

The Art of Short Selling, by Kathryn F. Staley [John Wiley & Sons, 1997; $34.95, hardcover].
Well written and thoroughly researched, this book will open your eyes to the perils of investing without doing thorough research, and it will teach you how to be a better analyst.

Classics: An Investor's Anthology [Business One Irwin, 1988, hardcover] and *Classics II: Another Investor's Anthology* [Irwin Professional Publishing, 1991; $50, hardcover], by Charles D. Ellis and James R. Vertin.

Though *Classics* is out of print and may be hard to find, it and its sequel, *Classics II,* include some of the finest articles ever written about investing. Reading these books will make you a seasoned veteran.

Common Stocks and Uncommon Profits and Other Writings, by Philip A. Fisher [John Wiley & Sons, 1996; $19.95].

According to press sources, this book had a huge influence on Warren Buffett. Enough said.

A Commonsense Guide to Mutual Funds, by Mary Rowland [Bloomberg Personal Bookshelf, 1996; $19.95, hardcover].

Mary Rowland is one of the few people writing about mutual funds today who has been doing it for more than 10 years. Her guide contains much of the wisdom she's gleaned from meeting hundreds of great and not-so-great investors. It's a quick read that will probably improve your investment results.

The Guide to Understanding Financial Statements, by Geza Szurovy and S.B. Costales [McGraw-Hill, 1993; $14.95].

About as easy to read as accounting books get. It is short, to the point, and has great instructions for creating a spreadsheet to calculate important ratios.

Hoover's Handbook of American Business, edited by Patric J. Spain and James R. Talbot [Hoover's Inc., 1996; $79.95, 2-vol. set, hardcover].

Hoover's provides great descriptions and history on a large number of companies. It should be available in most public libraries.

How to Buy Technology Stocks, by Michael Gianturco [Little Brown & Co., 1996; $13.95].
Gianturco does an excellent job explaining how investors can make profits in tech stocks without betting the farm.

How to Make Money in Stocks, by William J. O'Neil [McGraw-Hill, 1994; $10.95].
I've told you that *Investor's Business Daily* is one of the best sources for learning about small stocks. O'Neil's book will teach you how to use all of the tables of information in *IBD* to improve your investing.

The Intelligent Investor, by Benjamin Graham [Harper-Collins, 1997; $30.00, hardcover].
One of the greatest investing books of all time. You should read it every five years.

Market Timing for the Nineties, by Stephen Leeb and Roger S. Conrad [HarperCollins, 1994; $12.50].
Offers some commonsense market indicators.

The Market Wizards [HarperCollins, 1993; $15.00] and *The New Market Wizards* [John Wiley & Sons, 1995; $34.95, hardcover], by Jack D. Schwager.
Even if you never intend to be an active trader, you will become a better and more confident investor by reading these books.

Midas Investing, by Jonathan Steinberg [Times Books, 1996; $23.00, hardcover].
This brand-new book from the editor of *Individual Investor* magazine is a good handbook on investing in momentum stocks.

The Money Masters [HarperCollins, 1994; $14.00] and *The New Money Masters* [Harperperennial Library, 1994; $14.00], by John Train.
Interviews with some of the best money managers.

Nelson's Directory of Investment Research [Nelson Publications, 1995; $535.00].

One Up on Wall Street, by Peter Lynch [Penguin USA, 1990; $12.95].
I recommend this and anything else Lynch writes or has written. The guy is a genius.

Options As a Strategic Investment, by Lawrence G. McMillan [NY Institute of Finance, 1992; $49.95, hardcover].
If you really want to invest in options, you better read this book first.

Point & Figure Charting, by Thomas J. Dorsey [John Wiley & Sons, 1995; $55.00 hardcover].
If you think technical analysis is a bunch of baloney, you should read Dorsey's book. Dorsey believes that picking the most solid businesses won't necessarily make you money, since about three quarters of the risk in a stock comes from the market and the industry. He reduces his risk by studying supply and demand.

A Random Walk Down Wall Street, by Burton G. Malkiel [W.W. Norton & Co., 1996; $15.95].
Read this book. It tells you everything you'd get from an MBA course in finance, but in a far more lively style. Malkiel also outlines strategies you can put to work.

Security Analysis, by Benjamin Graham and David L. Dodd [McGraw-Hill, 1997; $50.00, hardcover].

The "holy book" of investing. I won't promise that you'll enjoy reading it or that you'll be able to get through it quickly, but it will really teach you to invest like a pro.

Small Cap Stocks, edited by Robert A. Klein and Jess Lederman [Probus Publishing Co., 1993; $70.00, hardcover].

This book contains some fantastic research on the small-cap market. It's a must-read for pros, but it would bore most amateurs.

Standard & Poor's SmallCap 600 Guide [McGraw-Hill, 1997; $24.95].

A very good source on small-cap stocks.

Value Investing Made Easy, by Janet Lowe [McGraw-Hill, 1996; $22.95, hardcover].

A nice little book about Benjamin Graham's life and value investing.

Walker's Manual of Unlisted Stocks [Walker's Manual Llc., 1996; $75.00, hardcover].

The manual, which you can order by calling (800) 932-2922, contains four years of financial data on 500 penny stocks. Read it before you put any money into that market.

What Works on Wall Street, by James P. O'Shaughnessy [McGraw-Hill, 1996; $29.95, hardcover].

A great book that explains which investing strategies beat the market over the long haul.

A Zebra in Lion Country, by Ralph Wanger [Simon & Schuster, 1997; $25.00, hardcover].

Wanger is one of the great small-cap investors, and a highly entertaining guy. I'm sure you'll want to read this book.

Newsletters
and Magazines

Barron's. Many market professionals consider *Barron's* a must-read for information on all the markets (800-328-6800, ext. 550).

Bloomberg Personal. As an editor, I'm obviously biased toward *Personal.* It contains interviews with and articles by many of the people mentioned in this book. You'll also find stocks that meet some of the investing criteria described here (888-432-5820).

Charles Schwab Mutual Funds Performance Guide. A comprehensive listing of small-cap funds (800-435-4000).

Individual Investor. One of the only magazines that concentrates on small stocks. I like the fact that the editors provide lots of thoroughly researched ideas in each issue. But don't forget that you need to follow up their research with your own (800-383-5901).

Investor's Business Daily. A great source for both stock and fund investors. If you include the paper's special features in your investment analysis and idea generating, your results will improve (800-831-2525).

Kiplinger's Personal Finance Magazine. Kiplinger's is a simple, no-nonsense magazine, containing lots of good ideas for managing your finances. Editor Fred Frailey also does great interviews (800-544-0155).

Morningstar Mutual Funds. This loose-leaf binder of 1,600 funds is a great source of mutual fund information. But you pay for what you get. Get your local library to subscribe if it doesn't already. You may be able to get Morningstar reports from your broker or from a fund you are planning to invest in. The company also publishes a monthly newsletter, Morningstar Investor (800-876-5005).

Mutual Funds. I started subscribing to this magazine because the subscription rate was really low, about $10. Now I learn something every time I thumb through (800-442-9000).

The No-Load Fund Investor. Sheldon Jacobs, a longtime observer of the mutual fund industry, covers new funds and provides recommendations and suggested portfolios (914-693-7420).

Oberweis Report. Always one of the top-ranked investment newsletters. Its picks have returned more than 28 percent a year since 1976 (630-801-6000).

The Red Chip Review. Marc Robins and his staff really dig to uncover great small companies that nobody else is following. You wouldn't believe how many pros speak highly of this report. It's also good to see that almost everyone on the staff is working to earn the Chartered Financial Analyst designation (503-241-1265, or 800-RedChip/800-838-9248).

SmartMoney. Here's another one to read on your trips to the library. It carries a regular feature on small-cap stocks once a year but doesn't devote much ink to companies with market caps below $500 million. Features on other areas of finance win lots of industry awards, though (800-444-4204).

Value Line Investment Survey. A compendium of one-page company reports published by Value Line, which ranks stocks according to safety and projected performance (800-833-0046).

Vickers Weekly Insider Report (800-645-5043) and *Insiders' Chronicle* (800-243-2324). Two newsletters that give you a window on insider buying and selling.

WEB SITES

THE INTERNET IS SHAPING UP as an extremely valuable source of investment advice. It seems like a new Web page pops up every day. I'll warn you right away, though, that you can't trust everything you read in print and you really can't trust everything you see on the Net. Some sites—like Bloomberg's and those run by our competitors Dow Jones, Standard & Poor's, and Reuters—should provide reliable information. I can vouch for the quality of Bloomberg's data, which is one of the things I really like about the site. There are other so-called information providers, though, that are merely mouthpieces companies pay to tout their stocks. So watch out for deception or just plain inaccuracy.

You should find helpful information at these addresses:

www.bloomberg.com Run by Bloomberg Financial Markets; provides news along with comprehensive stock and bond info.

www.cda.com CDA Investment publishes information on insider buying and selling.

www.dorseywright.com Dorsey, Wright & Associates' site can fill you in on point-and-figure technical analysis.

www.nasdaq.com Run by Nasdaq; provides price quotes.

www.pirc.com Run by the Primark Investment Research Center; publishes a list of companies announcing positive earnings surprises.

www.quote.com/info/vickers.html Vickers Insider Trade Report Service tattles on insider trading.

www.russell.com The Frank Russell Co., which compiles the Russell 2000 index of small-cap stocks, publishes asset allocation and market performance information on this Web site.

www.sec.gov/edgarhp.htm Edgar (Electronic Data Gathering, Analysis, and Retrieval).

www.stockinfo.standardpoor.com Standard & Poor's Reports-on-Demand service.

www.wsbi.com/spweb Run by Standard & Poor's Investor Center; offers tons of stock info you can download.

www.zacks.com Run by Zacks Investment Research; will conduct stock searches for $150 a year.

REGIONAL BROKERS

REGIONAL FIRMS CAN BE a good source for ideas. Here are the names of some that were highly ranked in *The Wall Street Journal's* February 1997 survey of investment houses' stock-picking prowess.

Raymond James and Associates, St. Petersburg, FL: (813) 573-3800

A.G. Edwards & Sons, St. Louis, MO: (314) 955-3000

Everen Securities, Chicago, IL: (312) 574-6000

Edward D. Jones, St. Louis, MO: (314) 515-2000

Piper Jaffray, Minneapolis, MN: (612) 342-6000

Wheat First, Richmond, VA: (804) 649-2311

PERMISSIONS CREDITS

APPENDIX

TICKER	COMPANY NAME	ADDRESS
AIR	AAR Corp	1111 Nicholas Blvd., Elk Grove Villg., IL 60007
ABM	ABM Indust. Inc	50 Fremont St., San Francisco, CA 94105
AMI	Acme Metals Inc	13500 S. Perry Ave., Riverdale, IL 60627
ACXM	Acxiom Corp	301 Industrial Blvd., Conway, AR 72033
ADAC	ADAC Labs	540 Alder Dr., Milpitas, CA 95035
ATIS	Advanced Tissue Sciences Inc	10933 N. Torrey Pines Rd., La Jolla, CA 92037
AD	ADVO Inc	1 Univac La., P.O. Box 755, Windsor, CT 06095
AG	AGCO Corp	4830 River Green Pkwy., Duluth, GA 30136
AWT	Air & Water Tech	3040 US Hwy. 22 W., Branchburg, NJ 08876
AEIC	Air Express Intl CP	120 Tokeneke Rd., Darien, CT 06820
AB	Alex Brown Inc	1 South St., Baltimore, MD 21202
ALN	Allen Group	25101 Chagrin Blvd., Beachwood, OH 44122
ALLP	Alliance Pharm. CP	3040 Science Pk. Rd., San Diego, CA 92121
ATK	Alliant Techsystems Inc	600 Second St. NE, Hopkins, MN 55343
GRP	Allied Group Inc	701 Fifth Ave., Des Moines, IA 50391
ALW	Allwaste Inc	5151 San Felipe, Houston, TX 77056
ALO	Alpharma Inc	1 Executive Dr., Fort Lee, NJ 07024
AIZ	Amcast Indl Corp	7887 Wash. Village Dr., Dayton, OH 45459
ACOL	AMCOL Intl Corp	1500 West Shure Dr., Arlington Hts., IL 60004
ABIG	Amer. Bankers Insur	11222 Quail Roost Dr., Miami, FL 33157
AFWY	Amer. Freightways	2200 Forward Dr., Harrison, AR 72601
AMSY	Amer. Mgmt. Sys.	4050 Legato Rd., Fairfax, VA 22033
EMT	Amer. Medical Response	2821 South Parker Rd., Aurora, CO 80014
AMMB	Amresco Inc	700 N. Pearl St., Dallas, TX 75201
AMTC	Amtech Corp	17304 Preston Rd., Bldg E100, Dallas, TX 75252
AGL	Angelica Corp	424 S. Woods Mill Rd., Chesterfield, MO 63017

COMPANIES THAT WERE members of the S&P 600
SmallCap Index as of 2/10/97

PHONE	WEB ADDRESS AS OF 2/10/97	INDUSTRY SUBGROUP
847-439-3939		Aerospace/Defense-Equip
415-597-4500	www.abm.com	Building-Maint/Service
708-849-2500		Steel-Producers
501-336-1000	www.acxiom.com	Data Processing/Mgmt
408-321-9100	www.adaclabs.com	Medical Imaging Systems
619-450-5730		Medical-Biomed/Gene
860-285-6100		Direct Mktg
770-813-9200		Machinery-Farm
908-685-4600		Environ Consulting/Eng
203-655-7900	www.aeilogis.com	Transport-Air Freight
410-727-1700	www.alexbrown.com	Finance-Invest Bnkr/Brkr
216-765-5800	www.allengroup.com	Telecomm Equip
619-558-4300	www.allp.com	Medical-Biomed/Gene
612-931-6000	www.atk.com	Firearms/Ammunition
515-280-4211	www.cfonews.com/algr	Property/Casualty Insur
713-623-8777	www.allwaste.com	Hazardous Waste Dispsl
201-947-7774	www.alpharma.com	Medical-Generic Drugs
937-291-7000	www.amcast.com	Metal Proc/Fabrica
847-394-8730	www.amcol.com	Metal-Diversified
305-253-2244	www.abig.com	Multi-line Insurance
501-741-9000		Transport-Truck
703-267-8000	www.amsinc.com	Computer Services
303-614-8500		Commercial Services
214-953-7700	www.amresco.com	Finance-Other Services
972-733-6600		Computers-Intgrtd Syst
314-854-3800		Linen Supply/Rel Items

TICKER	COMPANY NAME	ADDRESS
AXE	Anixter Intl Inc	2 N. Riverside Plz., Chicago, IL 60606
APOG	Apogee Enterprises	7900 Xerxes Ave. S., Minneapolis, MN 55431
APPB	Applebees Intl Inc	4551 W. 107th St., Ste. 100, Overland Park, KS 66207
ATR	AptarGroup Inc	475 W. Terra Cotta Ave., Crystal Lake, IL 60014
WTR	Aquarion Co	835 Main St., Bridgeport, CT 06604
ARBR	Arbor Drugs Inc	3331 W. Big Beaver, Troy, MI 48084
ACAT	Arctic Cat Inc	600 Brooks Ave. S., Thief River Falls, MN 56701
ABFS	Arkansas Best Corp	3801 Old Greenwood Rd., Fort Smith, AR 72903
ASHW	Ashworth Inc	2791 Loker Ave. West, Carlsbad, CA 92008
ASPT	Aspect Telecomm.	1730 Fox Dr., San Jose, CA 95131
ASTE	Astec Industries Inc	4101 Jerome Ave., Chattanooga, TN 37407
ASFC	Astoria Financial	1 Astoria Fed'l Plz., Lake Success, NY 11042
ATO	Atmos Energy Corp	5430 LBJ Freeway, Ste. 160, Dallas, TX 75240
ABPCA	Au Bon Pain Co Inc	19 Fid Kennedy Ave., Boston, MA 02210
ASPX	Auspex Sys. Inc	5200 Grt. Amer. Pkwy., Santa Clara, CA 95054
ASM	Authentic Fitness	6040 Bandini Blvd., Commerce, CA 90040
AZR	Aztar Corp	2390 E. Camelback Rd., Phoenix, AZ 85016
JBAK	Baker (J.) Inc	555 Turnpike St., Canton, MA 02021
BEZ	Baldor Electric	5711 RS Boreham Jr St., Fort Smith, AR 72908
BMP	Ballard Med. Prod.	12050 Lone Peak Pkwy., Draper, UT 84020
BTC	BancTec Inc	4435 Spring Valley Rd., Dallas, TX 75244
BGR	Bangor Hydro-Electr	33 State St., Bangor, ME 04401
BNYN	Banyan Sys. Inc	120 Flanders Rd., Westboro, MA 01581
BRR	Barrett Resources	1515 Arapahoe St.,Tower 3, Denver, CO 80202
BSET	Bassett Furniture Inds	Main St., Bassett, VA 24055
BBN	BBN Corp	150 Cambridge Pk. Dr., Cambridge, MA 02140
BEAV	BE Aerospace Inc	1400 Corp. Cntr. Way, Wellington, FL 33414
BI	Bell Industries Inc	11812 San Vicente Blvd., Los Angeles, CA 90049
BSPT	Bell Sports Corp	15170 N. Hayden, Ste. 1, Scottsdale, AZ 85260
BHE	Benchmark Elctrncs	3000 Technology Dr., Angleton, TX 77515
BNTN	Benton Oil & Gas Co	1145 Eugenia Pl., Carpinteria, CA93013
BERT	Bertucci's, Inc	14 Audubon Rd., Wakefield, MA 01880
BIR	Birmingham Steel	1000 Urban Cntr. Pkwy, Birmingham, AL 35242
BSYS	BISYS Group Inc	150 Clove Rd., Little Falls, NJ 07424
BMC	BMC Inds Inc-Minn	2 Appletree Sq., Minneapolis, MN 55425

PHONE	WEB ADDRESS AS OF 2/10/97	INDUSTRY SUBGROUP
312-902-1515	www.anixter.com	Wire/Cable Products
612-835-1874		Glass Products
913-967-4000	www.applebees.com	Retail-Restaurants
815-477-0424		Containers-Paper/Plastic
203-335-2333		Water
810-643-9420	www.arbordrugs.com	Retail-Drug Store
218-681-8558		Recreational Vehicles
501-785-6000	www.abfs.com	Transport-Truck
619-438-6610	www.golfman.com	Apparel Manufacturers
408-325-2200	www.aspect.com	Telecomm Equip
423-867-4210		Machine-Constr/Mining
516-327-3000		S&L/Thrifts-Eastern US
972-934-9227	www.atmosenergy.com	Gas-Distribution
617-423-2100	www.boston.com/aubonpain	Retail-Restaurants
408-986-2000	www.auspex.com	Networking Products
213-726-1262		Textile-Products
602-381-4100		Casino Hotels
617-828-9300		Retail-Apparel/Shoe
501-646-4711	www.industry.net/baldor	Machinery-Electrical
801-572-6800	www.bmed.com	Medical Products
972-450-7700	www.banc-tec.com	Optical Recognition Soft
207-945-5621		Electric-Integrated
508-898-1000	www.banyan.com	Network Software
303-572-3900		Oil Comp-Explor/Prodtn
540-629-6000	www.bassettfurniture.com	Home Furnishings-Orig
617-873-2000	www.bbn.com	Networking Products
561-791-5000	www.beav.com	Aerospace/Defense-Equip
310-826-2355	www.bellind.com	Electronic Parts Distrib
602-951-0033	www.bellsports.com	Leisure/Rec Products
409-849-6550		Electronic Compo-Misc
805-566-5600	www.bentonoil.com	Oil Comp-Explor/Prodtn
617-246-6700		Retail-Restaurants
205-970-1200		Steel-Producers
201-812-8600	www.bisys.com	Computer Services
612-851-6000		Electronic Compo-Misc

TICKER	COMPANY NAME	ADDRESS
BMCW	BMC West Corp	1475 Tyrell La., Boise, ID 83706
BBA	Bombay Comp. (The)	550 Bailey Ave., Fort Worth, TX 76107
BAMM	Books-A-Million Inc	402 Industrial La., Birmingham, AL 35211
BOOL	Boole & Babbage	3131 Zanker Rd., San Jose, CA 95134
BNE	Bowne & Co Inc	345 Hudson St., New York, NY 10014
BOXXB	Box Energy Corp	8201 Preston Rd., Dallas, TX 75225
BDT	Breed Technologies	5300 Old Tampa Hwy., Lakeland, FL 33811
BBTK	Broadband Technologies Inc	4024 Stirrup Creek Dr., P.O. Box 13737, Durham, NC 27709
BROD	Broderbund Software	500 Redwood Blvd.,Novato, CA 94948
BG	Brown Group Inc	8300 Maryland Ave., St. Louis, MO 63105
BBR	Butler Mfg Co	31st SW Trafficway, Kansas City, MO 64108
BWF	BW/IP Inc	200 Oceangate Blvd., Long Beach, CA 90802
CCBL	C-COR Electronics	60 Decibel Rd., State College, PA 16801
COG	Cabot Oil & Gas	15375 Memorial Dr., Houston, TX 77079
CGNE	Calgene Inc	1920 Fifth St., Davis, CA 95616
CMIC	California Microwave	555 Twin Dolphin Dr., Redwood City, CA 94065
CBM	Cambrex Corp	1 Meadowlands Plz., E. Rutherford, NJ 07073
CAM	Camco Intl Inc	7030 Ardmore, Houston, TX 77054
KRE	Capital RE Corp	1325 Ave. of the Americas, New York, NY 10019
CSAR	Caraustar Ind. Inc	3100 Washington St., Austell, GA 30001
CKE	Carmike Cinemas Inc	1301 First Ave., Columbus, GA 31901
CRP	Carson Pirie Scott	331 W. Wisconsin Ave., Milwaukee, WI 53203
CGC	Cascade Nat.Gas Corp	222 Fairview Ave. N., Seattle, WA 98109
CASY	Casey's Gen'l Stores	1 Convenience Blvd., Ankeny, IA 50021
PWN	Cash America Investments Inc	1600 W. 7th St., Fort Worth, TX 76102
CMAG	Casino Magic Corp	711 Casino Magic Dr., Bay St. Louis, MS 39520
CAS	Castle (A.M.) & Co	3400 N. Wolf Rd., Franklin Park, IL 60131
POS	Catalina Mktg. Corp	11300 Ninth St. N., St. Petersburg, FL 33716
CACOA	Cato Corp	8100 Denmark Rd., Charlotte, NC 28273
CCB	CCB Financial Corp	111 Corcoran St., Durham, NC 27702
CDI	CDI Corp	1717 Arch St., Philadelphia, PA 19103
CPRO	CellPro Inc	22215 26th Ave. SE, Bothell, WA 98021
CGRM	Centigram Comms.	91 E. Tasman Dr., San Jose, CA 95134

PHONE	WEB ADDRESS AS OF 2/10/97	INDUSTRY SUBGROUP
208-331-4410		Bldg Products-Ret/Whsle
817-347-8200	www.bombayco.com	Retail-Home Furnishings
205-942-3737		Retail-Bookstore
408-526-3000	www.boole.com	Computer Software
212-924-5500	www.bowne.com	Printing-Commercial
214-890-8000		Oil Comp-Explor/Prodtn
813-284-6000	www.breedtech.com	Auto/Trk Prts/Equip-Orig
919-544-0015	www.bbt.com	Telecomm Equip
415-382-4400	www.broderbund.com	Computer Software
314-854-4000	www.browngroup.com	Retail-Apparel/Shoe
816-968-3000	www.butlermfg.com	Bldg/Const. Prod-Misc
310-435-3700	www.bwip.com	Instruments-Controls
814-238-2461	www.c-cor.com	Electronic Compo-Misc
713-589-4600	www.cabotog.com	Oil/Gas Drilling
916-753-6313	www.calgene.com	Agricultural Biotech
415-596-9000	www.calmike.com	Telecomm Equip
201-804-3000		Chemicals-Diversified
713-747-4000		Oil Field Mach/Equip
212-974-0100		Financial Guarantee Ins
770-948-3101		Paper/Related Products
706-576-3400		Theaters
414-347-4141	www.carsons.com	Retail-Major Dept Store
206-624-3900		Gas-Distribution
515-965-6100	www.caseys.com	Retail-Convenience Store
817-335-1100		Retail-Pawn Shops
601-467-9257	www.casinomagic.com	Gambling (Non-Hotel)
847-455-7111		Metal Products-Distrib
813-579-5000	www.catalinamktg.com	Direct Mktg
704-554-8510		Retail-Apparel/Shoe
919-683-7777		Commer Banks-So US
215-569-2200		Engineer/R&D Services
206-485-7644	www.cellpro.com	Medical-Biomed/Gene
408-944-0250	www.centigram.com	Telecomm Equip

TICKER	COMPANY NAME	ADDRESS
CNH	Central Hudson Gas & Electric	284 South Ave., Poughkeepsie, NY 12601
CV	Central Vermont Public Service	77 Grove St., Rutland, VT 05701
CBC	Centura Banks Inc	134 N. Church St., Rocky Mount, NC 27804
CEPH	Cephalon Inc	145 Brandywine Pkwy., W. Chester, PA 19380
CERN	Cerner Corp	2800 Rockcreek Pkwy., Kansas City, MO 64117
CHB	Champion Enterprises Inc	2701 University Dr., Ste. 320, Auburn Hills, MI 48326
COFI	Charter One Fin Inc	1215 Superior Ave. NE, Cleveland, OH 44114
CAKE	Cheesecake Factory	26950 Agoura Rd., Calabasas Hills, CA 91301
CHE	Chemed Corp	2600 Chemed Cntr., 255 E. 5th St. Cincinnati, OH 45202
CEM	ChemFirst Inc	700 North St., P.O.B.1249, Jackson, MS 39215
CHPS	Chips & Technols. Inc	2950 Zanker Rd., San Jose, CA 95134
CQB	Chiquita Brands Intl	250 E. Fifth St., Cincinnati, OH 45202
CER	Cilcorp Inc	300 Hamilton Blvd., Ste. 300, Peoria, IL 61602
CPX	Cineplex Odeon Corp	1303 Yonge St., Toronto, Ont. M4T 2Y9, Can.
CCON	Circon Corp	6500 Hollister Ave., Santa Barbara, CA 93117
CKR	CKE Restaurant Inc	1200 N. Harbor Blvd., Anaheim, CA 92801
CLC	Clarcor Inc	2323 Sixth St., P.O.B. 7007, Rockford, IL 61125
CMT	CMAC Invstmnt	1601 Market St., 12 Fl., Philadelphia, PA 19103
CSA	Coast Savings Financial Inc	1000 Wilshire Blvd., Los Angeles, CA 90017
COKE	Coca-Cola Bottling	1900 Rexford Rd., Charlotte, NC 28211
CDE	Coeur d'Alene Mines	505 Front Ave., Coeur d'Alene, ID 83814
CGNX	Cognex Corp	1 Vision Dr., Natick, MA 01760
COHR	Coherent Inc	5100 Patrick Henry Dr., Santa Clara, CA 95054
CGEN	Collagen Corp	2500 Farber Pl., Palo Alto, CA94303
COFD	Collective Bancorp Inc	158 Philadelphia Ave. Egg Harbor City, NJ 08215
COMR	Comair Holdings Inc	P. O. Box 75021, Cincinnati Intl. Airport, Cincinnati, OH 45275
CFB	Commercial Federal Corp	2120 S. 72nd St., Omaha, NE 68101

PHONE	WEB ADDRESS AS OF 2/10/97	INDUSTRY SUBGROUP
914-452-2000	www.cenhud.com	Electric-Integrated
802-773-2711	www.cvps.com	Electric-Integrated
919-977-4400	www.centura.com	Commer Banks-So US
610-344-0200		Medical-Drugs
816-221-1024	www.cerner.com	Medical Information Sys
810-340-9090		Bldg-Mobil Hm/Mfd Hous
216-566-5300	www.charterone.com	S&L/Thrifts-Central US
818-880-9323		Retail-Restaurants
513-762-6900		Chemicals-Specialty
601-948-7550	www.chemfirst.com	Chemicals-Diversified
408-434-0600	www.chips.com	Elctrnc Compo-Semicon
513-784-8000	www.chiquita.com	Food-Misc/Diversified
309-675-8810	www.cilco.com	Electric-Integrated
416-323-6600		Theaters
805-685-5100	www.circoncorp.com	Medical Instruments
714-774-5796	www.ckr.com	Retail-Restaurants
815-962-8867	www.clarcor.com	Diversified Operations
215-564-6600	www.cmacmi.com	Financial Guarantee Ins
213-362-2000	www.coastfederal.com	S&L/Thrifts-Western US
704-551-4400	www.cocacola.com	Beverages-Non-alcoholic
208-667-3511	www.coeur.com/coeur/	Gold Mining
508-650-3000	www.cognex.com	Computers -Intgrtd Syst
408-764-4000	www.cohr.com	Lasers-Syst/Components
415-856-0200	www.collagen.com	Medical Instruments
609-625-1110		S&L/Thrifts-Eastern US
606-767-2550	www.fly-comair.com	Airlines
402-554-9200	www.comfedbank.com	S&L/Thrifts-Central US

TICKER	COMPANY NAME	ADDRESS
CMC	Commercial Metals Co	7800 Stemmons Freeway, P.O.B. 1046, Dallas, TX 75221
CELS	Commnet Cellular Inc	8350 E. Crescent Pkwy., Ste. 400, Englewood, CO 80111
CALC	Commonwealth Aluminum Corp	1200 Meidinger Tower, Louisville, KY 40202
CES	Commonwealth Energy Sys.	1 Main Street, Cambridge, MA 02142
CPDN	Compdent Corp	8800 Roswell Rd., Ste. 244, Atlanta, GA 30350
CLIX	Compression Labs	350 E. Plumeria Dr., San Jose, CA 95134
CPU	CompUSA Inc	14951 N. Dallas Pkwy., Dallas, TX 75240
CMVT	Comverse Technology	170 Crossways Pk. Dr.,Woodbury, NY 11797
COE	Cone Mills Corp	3101 N. Elm St., Greensboro, NC 27415
CNE	Conn. Energy Corp	855 Main St., Bridgeport, CT 06604
CONW	Consumers Water Co	Three Canal Plz., Portland, ME 04101
CON	Continental Homes Holding	7001 N. Scottsdale Rd., Ste. 2050, Scottsdale, AZ 85253
CDAT	Control Data Systems Inc	4201 N. Lexington Ave., Arden Hills, MN 55126
CORR	COR Therapeutics Inc	256 E. Grand Ave., S. San Francisco, CA 94080
CRI	Core Industries Inc	500 N. Woodward Ave., P. O. Box 2000, Bloomfield Hills, MI 48304
CXC	Corrections Corp of America	102 Woodmont Blvd., Nashville, TN 37205
CVTY	Coventry Corp	53 Century Blvd., Ste. 250, Nashville, TN 37214
ATX/A	Cross (A.T.) Company	1 Albion Rd., Lincoln, RI 02865
XTO	Cross Timbers Oil Co	810 Houston St., Ste. 2000, Ft. Worth, TX 76102
CFBI	Cullen/Frost Bankers	100 W. Houston St., San Antonio, TX 78205
CSTM	Custom Chrome Inc	16100 Jacqueline Ct., Morgan Hill, CA 95037
CYGN	Cygnus Inc	400 Penobscot Dr., Redwood City, CA 94063
CYRX	Cyrix Corp	2703 N. Centrl. Expwy., Richardson, TX 75080
CYRK	Cyrk Intl Inc	3 Pond Rd., Gloucester, MA 01930
DS	Dallas Semiconductor	4401 Beltwood Pkwy. S., Dallas, TX 75244
DMRK	Damark Intl Inc	7101 Winnetka Ave. N. Minneapolis, MN 55428
DM	Dames & Moore Inc	911 Wilshire Blvd., Los Angeles, CA 90017

PHONE	WEB ADDRESS AS OF 2/10/97	INDUSTRY SUBGROUP
214-689-4300		Metal Processors/Fabrica
303-694-3234	www.cels.com	Cellular Telecomm
502-589-8100		Metal-Aluminum
617-225-4000	www.comenergy.com	Electric-Integrated
770-998-8936		Life/Health Insurance
408-435-3000	www.clix.com	Telecomm Equip
972-982-4000	www.compusa.com	Retail-Consumer Electron
516-677-7200		Computers-Intgrtd Syst
910-379-6220		Textile-Products
203-579-1732	www.connenergy.com	Gas-Distribution
207-773-6438	www.consumerswater.com	Water
602-483-0006		Bldg-Residential/Commer
612-482-2401	www.cdc.com	Computer Services
415-244-6800		Medical-Biomed/Gene
810-642-3400	www.core-ind.com	Diversified Operations
615-292-3100		Protection-Safety
615-391-2440		Medical-HMO
401-333-1200		Office Supplies/Forms
817-870-2800		Oil Comp-Explor/Prodtn
210-220-4011	www.frostbank.com	Com Banks-Central US
408-778-0500		Leisure/Rec Products
415-369-4300		Drug Delivery Systems
972-968-8387	www.cyrix.com	Elctrnc Compo-Semicon
508-283-5800		Apparel Manufacturers
972-371-4000	www.dalsemi.com	Elctrnc Compo-Semicon
612-531-0066		Retail-Mail Order
213-683-1560		Pollution Control

TICKER	COMPANY NAME	ADDRESS
DAN	Daniel Industries	9753 Pine Lake Dr., Houston, TX 77055
SEEDB	Dekalb Genetics Corp	3100 Sycamore Rd., Dekalb, IL 60115
DLW	Delta Woodside Industries Inc	233 N. Main St., Hammond Sq., Ste. 200, Greenville, SC 29601
DEP	Deposit Guaranty Corp	210 E. Capitol St., P.O.B. 730 Jackson, MS 39205
DESI	Designs Inc	66 B St., Needham, MA 02194
DVN	Devon Energy Corp	20 N. Broadway, Oklahoma City, OK 73102
DV	Devry Inc	1 Tower La., Oakbrook Terrace, IL 60181
DGII	Digi Intl Inc	11001 Bren Rd. E., Minnetonka, MN 55343
DMIC	Digital Microwave	170 Rose Orchard Way, San Jose, CA 95134
DMN	Dimon Inc	512 Bridge St., P.O.B. 681, Danville, VA 24543
DNEX	Dionex Corp	1228 Titan Way, Sunnyvale, CA 94086
DAP	Discount Auto Parts	4900 Frontage Rd. S., Lakeland, FL 33815
DXYN	Dixie Yarns Inc	1100 S. Watkins St., Chattanooga, TN 37404
DSL	Downey Finan. Corp	3501 Jamboree Rd., Newport Beach, CA 92660
DRV	Dravo Corp	3600 One Oliver Plz., Pittsburgh, PA 15222
DBRN	Dress Barn Inc	30 Dunnigan Dr., Suffern, NY 10901
DYT	Dynatech Corp	3 New England Exec. Pk., Burlington, MA 01803
EAGL	Eagle Hrdw. & Grdn.	981 Powell Ave. SW, Renton, WA 98055
EGR	Earthgrains Co	8400 Maryland Ave., St. Louis, MO 63105
EUA	Eastern Utilities Assoc	1 Liberty Sq., Boston, MA 02109
EV	Eaton Vance Corp	24 Federal St., Boston, MA 02110
EGN	Energen Corp	2101 Sixth Ave. N. Birmimgham, AL 35203
EFS	Enhance Finl Svcs Gp.	335 Madison Ave., New York, NY 10017
ENVY	Envoy Corporation	2 Lakeview Pl., 15 Century Blvd., Ste. 600 Nashville, TN 37214
ENZ	Enzo Biochem Inc	60 Executive Blvd., Farmingdale, NY 11735
ETEC	Etec Systems Inc	26460 Corporate Ave., Hayward, CA 94545
ETH	Ethan Allen Interiors	Ethan Allen Dr., Danbury, CT 06811
EXPD	Expeditors Internatl. of Washington Inc	999 Third Ave., Ste. 2500, Seattle, WA 98104
ESRX	Express Scripts Inc	14000 Riverport Dr., Maryland Heights, MO 63043
FCA/A	Fabri-Centers of Amer	5555 Darrow Rd., Hudson, OH 44236
FIC	Fair Isaac & Company	120 N. Redwood Dr., San Rafael, CA 94903
FJC	Fedders Corp	505 Martinsville Rd., Liberty Corner, NJ 07938

PHONE	WEB ADDRESS AS OF 2/10/97	INDUSTRY SUBGROUP
713-467-6000	www.danielind.com	Oil Field Mach/Equip
815-758-3461	www.dekalb.com	Agricultural Operations
864-232-8301		Textile-Apparel
601-354-8497	www.dgb.com	Commer Banks-So US
617-444-7222		Retail-Apparel/Shoe
405-235-3611		Oil Comp-Explor/Prodtn
630-571-7700	www.devry.com	Human Resources
612-912-3444	www.dgii.com	Communication Software
408-943-0777	www.dmcwave.com	Fiber Optics
804-792-7511		Tobacco
408-737-0700	www.dionex.com	Instruments-Scientific
941-687-9226		Auto Parts-Retail/Whsle
423-698-2501		Textile-Products
714-854-0300	www.downeysavings.com	S&L/Thrifts-Western US
412-566-3000		BldgProd-Cement/Aggreg
914-369-4500		Retail-Apparel/Shoe
617-272-6100	www.dytc.com	Electronic Measur Instr
206-227-5740		Bldg Products-Ret/Whsle
314-259-7000		Food-Baking
617-357-9590	www.eua.com	Electric-Integrated
617-482-8260		Invest Mgmnt/Advis Serv
205 326-2700		Gas-Distribution
212-983-3100		Financial Guarantee Ins
615-885-3700	www.neic.com	Computer Services
516-755-5500		Medical-Biomed/Gene
510-783-9210	www.etec.com	Elctrnc Compo-Semicon
203-743-8000	www.ethanallen.com	Retail-Home Furnishings
206-674-3400	www.expd2.com	Transport-Air Freight
314-770-1666	www.expressscripts.com	Medical-HMO
216-656-2600		Retail-Fabric Store
415-472-2211	www.fairissac.com	Computer Services
908-604-8686		Air Conditioning

TICKER	COMPANY NAME	ADDRESS
FBD	Fibreboard Corp	2200 Ross Ave., Ste. 3600, Dallas, TX 75201
FNF	FIdelity Natl Finl Inc	17911 Von Karman Ave., Irvine, CA 92614
FLD	Fieldcrest Cannon	1 Lake Circle Dr., Kannapolis, NC 28081
FIGIA	Figgie Intl	4420 Sherwin Rd., Willoughby, OH 44094
BSMT	Filene's Basmnt Corp	40 Walnut St., Wellesley, MA 02181
FILE	Filenet Corp	3565 Harbor Blvd., Costa Mesa, CA 92626
FAF	First American Finl	114 E. Fifth St., Santa Ana, CA 92701
FCLR	First Commercial Corp	400 W. Capital Ave., P.O.B. 1471, Little Rock, AR 72201
FFHC	First Fin Corp-Wisc	1305 Main St., Stevens Point, WI 54481
FMBC	First Mich. Bank Corp	1 Financial Plz., Holland, MI 49423
FBP	Firstbank Puerto Rico	1519 Ponce de Leon Ave., Stop 23, Santurce, PR 00908
FMER	FirstMerit Corp	3 Cascade Plz., 7th Fl., Akron, OH44308
FSH	Fisher Scientific Intl	Liberty La., Hampton, NH 03842
FLOW	Flow Intl Corp	23500-64th Ave. S., Kent, WA 98032
FLK	Fluke Corp	6920 Seaway Blvd., Everett, WA 98203
FM	Foodmaker Inc	9330 Balboa Ave., San Diego, CA 92123
FNQ	Franklin Quest Co	2200 W. Pkwy. Blvd., Salt Lake City, UT 84119
FMT	Fremont General Corp	2020 Santa Monica Blvd., Ste. 600, Santa Monica, CA 90404
FRTZ	Fritz Companies Inc	706 Mission St., San Francisco, CA 94103
FTR	Frontier Insur Group	195 Lake Louise Marie Rd., Rock Hill, NY 12775
FFEX	Frozen Food Express Industries	1145 Empire Central Pl., Dallas, TX 75247
GKSRA	G & K Svcs. Inc	5995 Opus Pkwy., Minnetonka, MN 55343
GNL	Galey & Lord Inc	980 Ave. of the Americas, New York, NY 10018
AJG	Gallagher (Arthur J.)	2 Pierce Pl., Itasca, IL 60143
GAL	Galoob Toys Inc	500 Forbes Blvd., S. San Francisco, CA 94080
GCX	GC Companies Inc	27 Boylston St., Chestnut Hill, MA 02167
GHV	Genesis Health Ventures	148 West State St., Kennett Square, PA 19348
GNTX	Gentex Corp	600 N. Centennial St., Zeeland, MI 49464
GON	Geon Company	1 Geon Cntr., Avon Lake, OH 44012
GOTK	Geotek Comms. Inc	20 Craig Rd., Montvale, NJ 07645
GRB	Gerber Scientific Inc	83 Gerber Rd. West, South Windsor, CT 06074

PHONE	WEB ADDRESS AS OF 2/10/97	INDUSTRY SUBGROUP
214-954-9500		Bldg/Construct Prod
714-622-5000	www.fnf.com	Property/Casualty Ins
704-939-2000		Textile-Home Furnishings
216-953-2700		Diversified Operations
617-348-7000	www.interstep.com/basement	Retail-Discount
714-966-3400	www.filenet.com	Computer-Peripher Equip
714-558-3211	www.firstam.com	Property/Casualty Ins
501-371-7000	www.firstcommercial.com	Commer Banks-So. US
715-341-0400		S&L/Thrifts-Central US
616-355-9200	www.fmb.com	Commer Banks-Cntrl US
787-729-8200		Commer Banks-So US
330-996-6300		Commer Banks-Cntrl US
603-926-5911	www.fisher1.com	Instruments-Scientific
206-850-3500	www.flowcorp.com	Mach Tools/Rel Products
206-347-6100	www.fluke.com	Electronic Measur Instr
619-571-2121	www.foodmaker.com	Retail-Restaurants
801-975-1776		Computer Services
310-315-5500		Multi-line Insurance
415-904-8360	www.fritz.com	Transport-Services
914-796-2100		Property/Casualty Ins
214-630-8090	www.ffeinc.com	Transport-Truck
612-912-5500	www.gkcares.com	Linen Supply/Rel Items
212-465-3000		Textile-Products
630-773-3800	www.ajg.com	Insurance Brokers
415-952-1678	www.galoob.com	Toys
617-278-5600		Theaters
610-444-6350		Med-Outptnt/Home Med
616-772-1800	www.gentex.com	Auto/Trk Prts/Equip-Orig
216-930-1000	www.geon.com	Chemicals-Plastics
201-930-9305	www.geotek.com	Telecomm Services
860-644-1551	www.gerberscientific.com	Computer Services

TICKER	COMPANY NAME	ADDRESS
GGO	Getchell Gold Corp	5460 S. Quebec St., Englewood, CO 80111
GLG	Glamis Gold Ltd	3324 Four Bentall Centre 1055 Dunsmuir St., Vancouver, B.C., Canada V7X 1L3
GIX	Global Industrial Technologies Inc	2121 San Jacinto St., Ste. 2500, Dallas, TX 75201
GDMK	Goodmark Foods	6131 Falls of Neuse Rd., Raleigh, NC 27609
GOT	Gottschalks Inc	7 River Park Place. East, Fresno, CA 93720
GC	GranCare Inc	1 Ravinia Dr., Ste. 1500, Atlanta, GA 30346
GND	Grand Casinos Inc	130 Cheshire La., Minnetoka, MN 55305
GMP	Green Mtn. Pwr Corp	P.O.B. 85025, South Burlington, VT 05402
GFII	Greenfield Inds Inc	2743 Perimeter Pkwy., Augusta, GA 30909
GFF	Griffon Corp	100 Jericho Quadrangle, Jericho, NY 11753
GFD	Guilford Mills Inc	4925 W. Market St., Greensboro, NC 27407
HGGR	Haggar Corp	6113 Lemmon Ave., Dallas, TX 75209
HNH	Handy & Harman	250 Park Ave. New York, NY 10177
HRMN	Harmon Industries Inc	1300 Jefferson Ct., Blue Springs, MO 64015
HMX	Hartmarx Corp	101 N. Wacker Dr., Chicago, IL 60606
HAUS	Hauser Inc	5555 Airport Blvd., Boulder, CO 80301
HTLD	Heartland Express Inc	2777 Heartland Dr., Coralville, IA 52241
HECHA	Hechinger Co	1801 McCormick Dr., Largo, MD 20774
HL	Hecla Mining Co	6500 Mineral Dr., Coeur D'Alene, ID 83814
JKHY	Henry (Jack) & Assoc	663 W. Hwy. 60, Monett, MO 65708
HRH	Hilb Rogal&Hamilton	4235 Innslake Dr., Glen Allen, VA 23060
HPRK	Hollywood Park Inc	1050 S. Prairie Ave., Inglewood, CA 90301
HSE	HS Resources Inc	1 Maritime Plz., San Francisco, CA 94111
HUF	Huffy Corp	225 Byers Rd., Miamisburg, OH 45342
HUG	Hughes Supply Inc	20 N. Orange Ave., Orlando, FL 32801
HYSW	Hyperion Software	900 Long Ridge Rd., Stamford, CT 06902
IDXX	IDEXX Labs Inc	1 IDEXX Dr., Westbrook, ME 04092
IHOP	IHOP Corp	525 N. Brand Blvd., Glendale, CA 91203
IMR	IMCO Recycling Inc	5215 N. O'Connor Blvd., Irving, TX 75039
IMUL	ImmuLogic Pharm.	610 Lincoln St., Waltham, MA 02154
IMNR	Immune Response	5935 Darwin Ct., Carlsbad, CA 92008
IMD	IMO Industries Inc	1009 Lenox Dr., Lawrenceville, NJ 08648
IO	Input/Output Inc	11104 W. Airport Blvd., Stafford, TX 77477
INSUA	Insituform Technols.	1770 Kirby Pkwy., Ste. 300, Memphis, TN 38138

PHONE	WEB ADDRESS AS OF 2/10/97	INDUSTRY SUBGROUP
303-771-9000		Precious Metals
604-681-3541	www.glamis.com	Precious Metals
214-953-4500		Mach-Constr/Mining
919-790-9940		Food-Meat Products
209-434-8000	www.gotts.com	Retail-Regnl Dept Store
770-393-0199		Medical-Nursing Homes
612-449-9092	www.grandcasinos.com	Gambling (Non-Hotel)
802-864-5731	www.gmpvt.com	Electric-Integrated
706-863-7708	www.gfii.com	Mach Tools/Rel Products
516-938-5544		Diversified Operations
910-316-4000	www.guilfordmills.com	Textile-Products
214-352-8481		Apparel Manufacturers
212-661-2400		Precious Metals
816-229-3345		Electronic Compo-Misc
312-372-6300		Apparel Manufacturers
303-443-4662	www.hauser.com/hauser	Chemicals-Specialty
319-645-2728	www.heartlandexpress.com	Transp-Truck
301-341-1000		Bldg Products-Ret/Whsle
208-769-4100	www.hecla-mining.com	Precious Metals
417-235-6652	www.jackhenry.com	Computers-Intgrtd Sys
804-747-6500	www.hrh.com	Insurance Brokers
310-419-1500	www.racetech.com	Racetracks
415-433-5795	www.hsresources.com	Oil Comp-Explor/Prodtn
513-866-6251		Bicycle Manufacturing
407-841-4755	www.hughessupply.com	Bldg Products-Ret/Whsle
203-703-3000	www.hysoft.com	Data Processing/Mgmt
207-856-0300	www.idex.com	Medical Instruments
818-240-6055		Retail-Restaurants
972-869-6575		Recycling
617-466-6000		Medical-Biomed/Gene
619-431-7080	www.imnr.com	Medical-Drugs
609-896-7600		Instruments-Controls
281-933-3339	www.i-o.com	Oil Field Mach/Equip
901-759-7473		Building/Construct-Misc

TICKER	COMPANY NAME	ADDRESS
III	Insteel Industries	1373 Boggs Dr., Mount Airy, NC 27030
IAAI	Insur. Auto Auctions	1270 W. Northwest Hwy., Palatine, IL 60067
IN	Integon Corp/Del	500 W. Fifth St., Winston-Salem, NC 27152
ICST	Intgrtd. Circuit Sys.	2435 Blvd. of the Genrls., Valley Forge, PA 19482
IHS	Intgrtd. Health Svcs.	10065 Red Run Blvd., Owings Mills, MD 21117
IFSIA	Interface Inc	2859 Paces Ferry Rd., Atlanta, GA 30339
IS	Interim Svcs. Inc	2050 Spectrum Blvd., Ft. Lauderdale, FL 33309
IMG	Intermagnetics General Corp	450 Old Niskayuna Rd., P.O.B. 461, Latham, NY 12110
INMT	Intermet Corp	5445 Corporate Dr., Ste. 200, Troy, MI 48098
IFG	Interra Financial Inc	Dain Bosworth Plz., 60 S. Sixth St., Minneapolis, MN 55402
IBC	Interstate Bakeries	12 E. Armour Blvd., Kansas City, MO 64111
IPW	Interstate Power Co	1000 Main St., Dubuque, IA 52004
INTV	Intervoice Inc	17811 Waterview Pkwy., Dallas, TX 75252
FAM	Intl Fam. Entertainm.	2877 Guardian La., Virginia Beach, VA 23452
IRF	Intl Rectifier Corp	233 Kansas St., El Segundo, CA 90245
IVCR	Invacare Corp	899 Cleveland St., Elyria, OH 44035
ION	IONICS Inc	65 Grove St., Watertown, MA 02172
ITRI	ITRON Inc	2818 N. Sullivan Rd., Spokane, WA 99216
JJSF	J & J Snack Foods	6000 Central Hwy., Pennsauken, NJ 08109
JBM	Jan Bell Marketing	13801 NW 14th St., Sunrise, FL 33323
JII	Johnston Ind-Del	105 Thirteenth St., Columbus, GA 31901
JSBF	JSB Financial Inc	303 Merrick Rd., Lynbrook, NY 11563
WON	JumboSports Inc	4701 W. Hillsborough Ave., Tampa, FL 33614
JUNO	Juno Lighting Inc	2001 S. Mt. Prospect Rd., Des Plaines, IL 60017
JSTN	Justin Industries	2821 W. 7th St., Fort Worth, TX 76107
KNE	K N Energy Inc	370 Van Gordon St., Lakewood, CO 80228
KSWS	K-Swiss Inc	20664 Bahama St., Chatsworth, CA 91311
KTO	K2 Inc	4900 S. Eastern Ave., Los Angeles, CA 90040
KAMNA	Kaman Corp	1332 Blue Hills Ave., Bloomfield, CT 06002
KCS	KCS Energy Inc	379 Thornall St., Edison, NJ 08837
KEA	Keane Inc	Ten City Sq., Boston, MA 02129
KWD	Kellwood Co	600 Kellwood Pkwy., Chesterfield, MO 63017
KMET	Kemet Corp	2835 Kemet Way, Simpsonville, SC 29681
KNT	Kent Electronics Corp	7433 Harwin Dr., Houston, TX 77036

PHONE	WEB ADDRESS AS OF 2/10/97	INDUSTRY SUBGROUP
910-786-2141		Wire/Cable Products
847-705-9550	www.sandiego.sisna.com/iaa	Commercial Services
910-770-2000		Property/Casualty Ins
610-630-5300	www.icst.com	Elctrnc Compo-Semicon
410-998-8400	www.ihs-inc.com	Medical-Hospitals
770-437-6800	www.ifsia.com	Textile-Home Furnishings
954-938-7600	www.interim.com	Human Resources
518-782-1122		Superconductor Prod/Sys
810-952-2500		Auto/Trk Prts/Equip-Orig
612-371-7750		Finance-Invest Bnkr/Brkr
816-502-4000	www.irin.com/ibc	Food-Baking
319-582-5421		Electric-Integrated
972-454-8000	www.intervoice.com	Computers-Voice Recogn
757-459-6000	www.famfun.com	Cable TV
310-726-8000	www.irf.com	Electrnc Compo-Semicon
216-329-6000	www.invacare.com	Hospital Beds/Equipment
617-926-2500	www.ionics.com	Water Treatment Syst
509-924-9900	www.itron.com	Electronic Measur Instr
609-665-9533		Food-Misc/Diversified
954-846-2705		Precious Metals/Jewelry
706-641-3140		Textile-Products
516-887-7000		S&L/Thrifts-Eastern US
813-886-9688		Retail-Sporting Goods
847-827-9880		Bldg Prod-Light Fixtures
817-336-5125	www.justinind.com	Diversified Operations
303-989-1740	www.kne.com	Oil Refining/Mktg
818-998-3388	www.kswiss.com	Athletic Footwear
213-724-2800	www.k2sports.com	Leisure/Rec Products
860-243-7100	www.kaman.com	Aerospace/Defense-Equip
908-632-1770		Oil Comp-Explor/Prodtn
617-241-9200	www.keane.com	Data Processing/Mgmt
314-576-3100		Apparel Manufacturers
864-963-6300	www.kemet.com	Capacitors
713-780-7770	www.kentelec.com	Electronic Parts Distrib

TICKER	COMPANY NAME	ADDRESS
KSTN	Keystone Finl Inc	1 Keystone Plz., Harrisburg, PA 17101
KCLC	KinderCare Lrng. Ctrs	2400 Presidents Dr., Montgomery, AL 36116
KEX	Kirby Corp	1775 St. James Pl., Ste. 300, Houston, TX 77056
KMAG	Komag Inc	275 S. Hillview Dr., Milpitas, CA 95035
KRON	Kronos Inc	400 Fifth Ave., Waltham, MA 02154
KUH	Kuhlman Corp	3 Skidaway Village Sq., Savannah, GA 31411
KZ	Kysor Industrial Corp	1 Madison Ave., Cadillac, MI 49601
LZB	LA-Z-Boy Inc	1284 N. Telegraph Rd., Monroe, MI 48162
LSTR	Landstar System Inc	1000 Bridgeport Ave., Shelton, CT 06484
LSCC	Lattice Semiconduct.	5555 NE Moore Ct., Hillsboro, OR 97124
LECH	Lechters Inc	1 Cape May St., Harrison, NJ 07029
LM	Legg Mason Inc	111 S. Calvert St., Baltimore, MD 21202
LFI	Levitz Furniture Inc	6111 Broken Sound Parkway NW, Boca Raton, FL 33487
LBNA	Liberty Bancorp/Okl.	100 N. Broadway, Oklahoma City, OK 73102
LRE	Life Re Corp	969 High Ridge Rd., Stamford, CT 06905
LVC	Lillian Vernon Corp	543 Main St., New Rochelle, NY 10801
LI	Lilly Industries Inc	733 South West St., Indianapolis, IN 46225
LNCR	Lincare Holdings Inc	19337 US 19 N., Ste. 500, Clearwater, FL 34624
LINZ	Lindsay Manuf Co	East Hwy. 91, Lindsay, NE 68644
LIPO	Liposome Co Inc	1 Resrch. Way, Forrestal Ctr., Princeton, NJ 08540
LCA	Living Cntrs of Amer.	15415 Katy Freeway, Houston, TX 77094
LGN	Logicon Inc	3701 Skypark Dr., Torrance, CA 90505
LCE	Lone Star Industries	300 First Stamford Pl., Stamford, CT 06912
LSB	LSB Industries Inc	16 S. Pennsylvania Ave., Oklahoma City, OK 73107
LUB	Luby's Cafeterias Inc	2211 NE Loop 410, San Antonio, TX 78265
LDL	Lydall Inc	1 Colonial Rd., Manchester, CT 06040
MGL	Magellan Health Svcs	3414 Peachtree Rd. NE, Atlanta, GA 30326
MGR	Magna Group Inc	1401 S. Brentwood Blvd., St. Louis, MO 63144
MAIL	Mail Boxes Etc	6060 Cornerstone Ct. W., San Diego, CA 92121
MTW	Manitowoc Co	500 S. 16th St., Manitowoc, WI 54220
MCS	Marcus Corp	250 E. Wisconsin Ave., Milwaukee, WI 53202
MRNR	Mariner Health Grp	125 Eugene O'Neill Dr., New London, CT 06320
MTB	Mark Twain Bancshares Inc	8820 Ladue Rd., St. Louis, MO 63124
MI	Marshall Industries	9320 Telstar Ave., El Monte, CA 91731

PHONE	WEB ADDRESS AS OF 2/10/97	INDUSTRY SUBGROUP
717-233-1555	www.keyfin.com	Commer Banks-Eastrn US
334-277-5090	www.kindercare.com	Commercial Services
713-629-9370		Transport-Marine
408-946-2300	www.komag.com	Computers-Mem Devices
617-890-3232	www.kronos.com	Computers-Intgrtd Syst
912-598-7809		Machinery-Electric Util
616-779-2200	www.prosonline.com/kysor	Auto/Trk Prts/Equip-Orig
313-241-4414	www.lazyboy.com	Home Furnishings-Orig
203-925-2900	www.landstar.com	Transport-Truck
503-681-0118	www.latticesemi.com	Elctrnc Compo-Semicon
201-481-1100	www.lechters.com	Retail-Cutlery/Cookware
410-539-0000	www.leggmason.com	Finance-Invest Bnkr/Brkr
561-994-6006	www.levitz.com	Retail-Home Furnishings
405-231-6000	www.libertybank.com	Commer Banks-Cntrl US
203-321-3000		Life/Health Insurance
914-576-6400		Retail-Mail Order
317-687-6700	www.lillyindustries.com	Chemicals-Specialty
813-530-7700	www.lincare.com	Med-Outptnt/Home Med
402-428-2131		Machinery-Farm
609-452-7060	www.lipo.com	Medical-Biomed/Gene
281-578-4600		Medical-Nursing Homes
310-373-0220	www.logicon.com	Electronics-Military
203-969-8600		BldgProd-Cement/Aggreg
405-235-4546		Diversified Operations
210-654-9000	www.lubys.com	Retail-Restaurants
860-646-1233		Pollution Control
404-841-9200		Medical-Hospitals
314-963-2500	www.magnabank.com	Commer Banks-Cntrl US
619-455-8800	www.mbe.com	Retail-Misc/Diversified
414-684-4410	www.manitowoc.com	Machine-Constr/Mining
414-272-6020		Hotels/Motels
860-701-2000		Medical-Nursing Homes
314-727-1000	www.marktwain.com	Commer Banks-Cntrl US
818-307-6000	www.marshall.com	Elctrnc Compo-Semicon

TICKER	COMPANY NAME	ADDRESS
MSC	Material Sciences Crp	2300 E. Pratt Blvd., Elk Grove Village, IL 60007
MWT	McWhorter Techns.	400 E. Cottage Pl., Carpentersville, IL 60110
MDC	MDC Holdings Inc	3600 S. Yosemite St., Ste. 900, Denver, CO 80237
MEDI	MedImmune Inc	35 W. Watkins Mill Rd., Gaithersburg, MD 20878
MSA	Medusa Corp	3008 Monticello Blvd., Cleveland Hts., OH 44118
MNTR	Mentor Corp	5425 Hollister Ave., Santa Barbara, CA 93111
MRLL	Merrill Corporation	1 Merrill Cir., St., Paul, MN 55108
MESA	Mesa Air Group Inc	3753 Howard Hughes Pkwy., Ste. 200 Las Vegas, NV 89109
MXP	Mesa Inc	1400 Williams Sq. W., 5205 N. O'Connor Blvd., Irving, TX 75039
METHA	Methode Electronics	7444 W. Wilson Ave., Harwood Hts., IL 60656
MIKE	Michaels Stores Inc	8000 Bent Branch Dr., Irving, TX 75063
MICA	MicroAge Inc	2400 S. MicroAge Way, Tempe, AZ 85282
MCHP	Microchip Technlgy	2355 W. Chandler Blvd., Chandler, AZ 85224
MNPI	Microcom Inc	500 River Ridge Dr., Norwood, MA 02062
GRO	Mississippi Chemical	P.O.B. 388, Yazoo City, MS 39194
MOHK	Mohawk Indust. Inc	160 S. Industrial Blvd., Calhoun, GA 30701
MB	Molecular Biosys. Inc	10030 Barnes Canyon Rd., San Diego, CA 92121
MK	Morrison Knudsen	Morrison Knudsen Plz., Boise, ID 83729
MOSI	Mosinee Paper Corp	1244 Kronenwetter Dr., Mosinee, WI 54455
MSCA	MS Carriers Inc	3171 Directors Row, Memphis, TN 38131
MLI	Mueller Indust. Inc	6799 Great Oaks Rd., Memphis, TN 38138
MM	Mutual Risk Mgmt	44 Church St., Hamilton HM 12, Bermuda
MYCO	Mycogen Corp	5501 Oberlin Dr., San Diego, CA 92121
MYE	Myers Indust. Inc	1293 S. Main St., Akron, OH 44301
NAFC	Nash Finch Co	7600 France Ave. S., Ste. 200, Edina, MN 55435
NSH	Nashua Corp	44 Franklin St., Nashua, NH 03060
NAK	Nat. Auto Credit Inc	30000 Aurora Rd., Solon, OH 44139
NLCS	National Computer Systems Inc	11000 Prairie Lakes Dr., Eden Prairie, MN 55344
NDC	National Data Corp	National Data Plz., Atlanta, GA 30329
NATR	Nature's Sunshine Products Inc	75 E. 1700 South, Provo, UT 84606
NAUT	Nautica Enterprises	40 W. 57th St., New York, NY 10019
NBTY	NBTY Inc	90 Orville Dr., Bohemia, NY 11716

PHONE	WEB ADDRESS AS OF 2/10/97	INDUSTRY SUBGROUP
847-439-8270	www.matsci.com	Steel-Specialty
847-428-2657		Chemicals-Specialty
303-773-1100		Building/Construct-Misc
301-417-0770	www.medimmune.com	Medical-Biomed/Gene
216-371-4000		BldgProd-Cement/Aggreg
805-681-6000		Medical Products
612-646-4501	www.merrillcorp.com	Printing-Commercial
702-892-3773	www.mesa-air.com	Airlines
972-444-9001	www.mesainc.com	Oil Comp-Explor/Prodtn
708-867-9600	www.methode.com	Electronic Compo-Misc
972-409-1300	www.michaels.com	Retail-Arts/Crafts
602-804-2000	www.microage.com	Retail-Whsle Companies
602-786-7200	www.microchip.com	Instruments-Controls
617-551-1000	www.microcom.com	Networking Products
601-746-4131	www.misschem.com	Fertilizers
706-629-7721	www.mohawkcarpet.com	Textile-Home Furnishings
619-452-0681		Medical-Biomed/Gene
208-386-5000		Building-Heavy Construct
715-693-4470		Paper/Related Products
901-332-2500		Transport-Truck
901-753-3200		Metal Processors/Fabrica
441-295-5688	www.mutrisk.com	Property/Casualty Ins
619-453-8030	www.mycogen.com	Medical-Biomed/Gene
330-253-5592		Rubber/Plastics
612-832-0534		Food Items-Wholesale
603-880-2323	www.nashua.mv.com	Office Supplies/Forms
216-349-1000		Finance-Auto Loan Serv
612-829-3000	www.ncs.com	Optical Recognition Soft
404-728-2000		Data Processing/Mgmt
801-342-4300	www.natr.com	Cosmetics/Toiletries
212-541-5990		Apparel Manufacturers
516-567-9500		Cosmetics/Toiletries

TICKER	COMPANY NAME	ADDRESS
NWK	Network Eqpt. Techn	800 Saginaw Dr., Redwood City, CA 94063
NETG	Network General	4200 Bohannon Dr., Menlo Park, CA 94025
NEB	New England Business Svc Inc	500 Main St., Groton, MA 01471
NJR	N J Resources	1415 Wyckoff Rd., Wall, NJ 07719
NFX	Newfield Exploration Co	363 N. Sam Houston Pkwy. E., Ste. 2020, Houston, TX 77060
NFOR	NFO Research Inc	2 Pickwick Plz., Greenwich, CT 06830
NE	Noble Drilling Corp	10370 Richmond Ave., Houston, TX 77042
NRND	Norand Corp	550 Second St. SE Cedar Rapids, IA 52401
NRL	Norrell Corp	3535 Piedmont Rd. NE, Atlanta, GA 30305
NAC	North American Mortgage Co	3883 Airway Dr., Santa Rosa, CA 95403
NVX	North American Vaccine Inc	12103 Indian Creek Ct., Beltsville, MD 20705
NWNG	Northwest Nat. Gas	220 NW Second Ave.,Portland, OR 97209
NWSW	Northwestern Steel & Wire Co	121 Wallace St., Sterling, IL 61081
NVLS	Novellus Sys. Inc	3970 N. First St., San Jose, CA 95134
NOVN	Noven Phamaceutls.	11960 SW 144th St., Miami, FL 33186
NTN	NTN Comms. Inc	5966 La Place Ct., Carlsbad, CA 92008
ORLY	O'Reilly Automotive	233 S. Patterson Ave., Springfield, MO 65802
OSL	O'Sullivan Corp	1944 Valley Ave., Winchester, VA 22601
OAK	Oak Industries Inc	1000 Winter St., Waltham, MA 02154
OH	Oakwood Homes	7800 McCloud Rd., Greensboro, NC 27409
OII	Oceaneering Intl Inc	16001 Pk. Ten Pl., Ste. 600, Houston, TX 77084
OLOG	Offshore Logistics	224 Rue de Jean, Lafayette, LA 70508
OHM	OHM Corp	16406 U.S. Route 224 East, Findlay, OH 45840
OMP	OM Group Inc	50 Public Square, 3800 Terminal Tower, Cleveland, OH 44113
OMEG	Omega Environmental Inc	19805 N. Creek Pkwy., Bothell, WA 98011
OCR	Omnicare Inc	255 E. Fifth St., Cincinnati, OH 45202
ONBK	ONBANCorp Inc	101 S. Salina St., Syracuse, NY 13202
ORU	Orange & Rockland Utilities	1 Blue Hill Plz., Pearl River, NY 10965

PHONE	WEB ADDRESS AS OF 2/10/97	INDUSTRY SUBGROUP
415-366-4400	www.net.com	Telecomm Equip
415-473-2000	www.ngc.com	Network Software
508-448-6111	www.nebs.com	Office Supplies/Forms
908-938-1480	www.njng.com	Gas-Distribution
281-847-6000	www.newfld.com	Oil Comp-Explor/Prodtn
203-629-8888	www.nfor.com	Commercial Services
713-974-3131		Oil/Gas Drilling
319-369-3100	www.norand.com	Computers-Intgrtd Syst
404-240-3000	www.norrell.com	Human Resources
707-523-5000	www.namc.com	Fin-Mtge Loan/Banker
301-470-6100	www.nava.com	Medical-Drugs
503-226-4211	www.nng.com	Gas-Distribution
815-625-2500		Steel-Producers
408-943-9700		Elctrnc Compo-Semicon
305-253-5099		Medical-Drugs
619-438-7400	www.ntn.com	Cable TV
417-862-3333		Auto Parts-Retail/Whsle
540-667-6666	www.osul.com	Rubber/Plastics
617-890-0400		Electronic Compo-Misc
910-664-2400	www.oakwooodhomes.com	Mobil Home/Mfd Hous
281-578-8868	www.oceaneering.com	Oil-Field Services
318-233-1221		Transport-Services
419-423-3529	www.ohm.com	Hazardous Waste Dspsl
216-781-0083	www.omgi.com	Chemicals-Specialty
206-486-4800		Remediation Services
513-762-6666		Pharmacy Services
315-424-4400	www.onbank.com	S&L/Thrifts-Eastern US
914-352-6000	www.oru.com	Electric-Integrated

TICKER	COMPANY NAME	ADDRESS
ORBI	Orbital Sciences Corp	21700 Atlantic Blvd., Dulles, VA 20166
OC	Orion Capital Corp	600 Fifth Ave., New York, NY 10020
GOSHA	Oshkosh B'Gosh Inc	112 Otter Ave., Oshkosh, WI 54901
OM	Outboard Marine	100 Seahorse Dr.,Waukegan, IL 60085
OMI	Owens & Minor Inc	4800 Cox Rd., Glen Allen, VA 20360
OXM	Oxford Industries Inc	222 Piedmont Ave. NE, Atlanta, GA 30308
PSX	Pacific Scientific Co	620 Nwprt. Cntr. Dr., Newport Beach, CA 92660
PTB	Paragon Trade Brands Inc	180 Technology Pkwy., Norcross, GA 30092
PKE	Park Electrochemical	5 Dakota Dr., Lake Success, NY 11042
PDCO	Patterson Dental Co	1031 Mendota Heights Rd, St. Paul, MN 55120
PXR	PAXAR Corp	105 Corporate Pk. Dr., White Plains, NY 10604
PCS	Payless Cashways	2300 Main St.,Kansas City, MO 64108
PNT	Penn Enterprises Inc	39 Public Sq.,Wilkes-Barre, PA 18711
PENW	Penwest Ltd	777-108th Ave. NE, Bellevue, WA 98004
PBIO	PerSeptive Biosystems Inc	500 Old Connecticut. Path, Framingham, MA 01701
PMRX	Pharmaceutical Marketing Svs.	45 Rockefeller Plz., Ste. 912, New York, NY 10111
PRX	Pharmaceutical Resources Inc	1 Ram Ridge Rd., Spring Valley, NY 10977
PSC	Phila. Suburban Corp	762 Lancaster Ave., Bryn Mawr, PA 19010
PVH	Phillips-Van Heusen	1290 Ave. of the Americas, New York, NY 10104
PLAB	Photronics Inc	1061 E. Indiantown Rd., Jupiter, FL 33477
PHYC	PhyCor Inc	30 Burton Hills Blvd, Nashville, TN 37215
PCTL	PictureTel Corp	100 Minuteman Rd., Andover, MA 01810
PNY	Piedmont Nat. Gas	1915 Rexford Rd., Charlotte, NC 28211
PIR	Pier 1 Imports Inc	301 Commerce St., Fort Worth, TX 76102
PTX	Pillowtex Corp	4111 Mint Way, Dallas, TX 75237
PIOG	Pioneer Group Inc	60 State St., Boston, MA 02109
PIOS	Pioneer Standard Electronics	4800 East 131st Street, Cleveland, OH 44105
PJC	Piper Jaffrey Funds	222 S. Ninth St., Minneapolis, MN 55402
PZX	Pittston Burlington	1000 Virginia Cntr. Pkwy., Glen Allen, VA 23060
PLX	Plains Resources Inc	1600 Smith St., Ste. 1500, Houston, TX 77002
PSQL	Platinum Software	195 Technology Dr., Irvine, CA 92618

PHONE	WEB ADDRESS AS OF 2/10/97	INDUSTRY SUBGROUP
703-406-5000	www.orbital.com	Aerospace/Defense-Equip
212-332-8080		Property/Casualty Ins
414-231-8800		Apparel Manufacturers
847-689-6200	www.omc-online.com	Recreational Vehicles
804-747-9794		Medical Products
404-659-2424		Apparel Manufacturers
714-720-1714		Machinery-Electrical
770-300-4000		Paper/Related Products
516-354-4100	www.parkelectro.com	Circuit Boards
612-686-1600	www.pdental.com	Dental Supplies/Equip
914-697-6800	www.paxar.com	Machinery-Generl Indust
816-234-6000	www.payless.cashways.com	Bldg Products Ret/Whsle
717-829-8843		Gas-Distribution
206-462-6000	www.penw.com	Chemicals-Specialty
508-383-7700	www.pbio.com	Instruments-Scientific
212-841-0610		Commercial Services
914-425-7100		Medical-Generic Drugs
610-527-8000	www.suburbanwater.com	Water
212-541-5200		Apparel Manufacturers
561-745-1222	www.photronics.com	Elctrnc Compo-Semicon
615-665-9066	www.phycor.com	Health Care Cost Contain
508-292-5000	www.picturetel.com	Telecomm Equip
704-364-3120	www.piedmontng.com	Gas-Distribution
817-878-8000	www.pier1.com	Retail-Home Furnishings
214-333-3225	www.pillowtex.com	Textile-Home Furnishings
617-742-7825		Finance-Invest Bnkr/Brkr
216-587-3600	www.pios.com	Elctrnc Compo-Semicon
612-342-6000	www.piperjaffray.com	Finance-Invest Bnkr/Brkr
804-553-3600		Transport-Air Freight
713-654-1414		Oil Comp-Explor/Prodtn
714-453-4000	www.platsoft.com	Applications Software

TICKER	COMPANY NAME	ADDRESS
PLAT	Platinum Technlgy	815 S. Meyers Rd., Oakbrook Terr., IL 60181
PLAY	Players Intl Inc	1300 Atlantic Ave., Atlantic City, NJ 08401
PLEN	Plenum Publishing	233 Spring St., New York, NY 10013
PLXS	Plexus Corp	55 Jewelers Park Dr., Neenah, WI 54957
PGI	Ply Gem Industries	777 Third Ave., New York, NY 10017
PPP	Pogo Producing Co	5 Greenway Plz., Houston, TX 77046
PESC	Pool Energy Svcs. Co	10375 Richmond Ave., Houston, TX 77042
POP	Pope & Talbot Inc	1500 SW First Ave., Portland, OR 97201
PMI	Premark Intl Inc	1717 Deerfield Rd., Deerfield, IL 60015
PRDE	Pride Petroleum Svcs	1500 City West Blvd., Houston, TX 77042
PMK	Primark Corp	1000 Winter St., Waltham, MA 02154
PDQ	Prime Hospitality	700 Route 46 East, Fairfield, NJ 07004
PROP	Production Operators Corp	11302 Tanner Rd., Houston, TX 77041
PRFT	Proffitts Inc	115 N. Calderwood St., Alcoa, TN 37701
PRGS	Progress Software	14 Oak Park, Bedford, MA 01730
PL	Protective Life Corp	2801 Hwy. 280 South, Birmingham, AL 35223
PDLI	Protein Design Labs	2375 Garcia Avenue, Mountain View, CA 94043
PRBK	Provident Bancorp	1 E. Fourth St., Cincinnati, OH 45202
PGS	Public Svc. Co of NC	400 Cox Rd., Gastonia, NC 28054
KWR	Quaker Chemical Crp	Elm and Lee Streets, Conshohocken, PA 19428
NX	Quanex Corp	1900 West Loop S., Houston, TX 77027
BQR	Quick & Reilly Group	230 S. County Rd., Palm Beach, FL 33480
RTEX	Railtex Inc	4040 Broadway, San Antonio, TX 78209
RJF	Raymond James Financial Corp	880 Carillon Parkway, St. Petersburg, FL 33716
RCSB	RCSB Financial Inc	235 E. Main St., Rochester, NY 14604
RDM	RDM Sports Group	250 Spring St. NW, Atlanta, GA 30303
RDRT	Read-Rite Corp	345 Los Coches St., Milpitas, CA 95035
RBC	Regal Beloit	200 State St., Beloit, WI 53511
REGL	Regal Cinemas Inc	7132 Commercial Pk. Dr., Knoxville, TN 37918
REGN	Regeneron Pharmaceuticals	777 Old Saw Mill River Rd., Tarrytown, NY 10591
RGIS	Regis Corp	7201 Metro Blvd., Minneapolis, MN 55439
RGC	Republic Gypsum Co	811 E. 30th Ave., Hutchinson, KS 67502
RSND	Resound Corp	220 Saginaw Dr., Redwood City, CA 94063

PHONE	WEB ADDRESS AS OF 2/10/97	INDUSTRY SUBGROUP
630-620-5000	www.platinum.com	Computer Software
609-449-7777		Gambling (Non-Hotel)
212-620-8000		Publishing-Books
414-722-3451	www.plexus.com	Elctrnc Compo-Semicon
212-832-1550	www.plygem.com	Bldg/Construct Prod-Misc
713-297-5000		Oil Comp-Explor/Prodtn
713-954-3000		Oil-Field Services
503-228-9161	www.poptal.com	Paper/Related Products
847-405-6000	www.premarkintl.com	Retail-Cutlery/Cookware
713-789-1400	www.prde.com	Oil-Field Services
617-466-6611	www.primark.com	Computer Services
201-882-1010		Hotels/Motels
713-466-0980		Oil-Field Services
423-983-7000	www.proffitts.com	Retail-Regnl Dept Store
617-280-4000	www.progress.com	Applications Software
205-879-9230	www.protective.com	Life/Health Insurance
415-903-3700	www.pdl.com	Medical-Biomed/Gene
513-345-7102	www.cin.ix.net/provident	Commer Banks-Cntrl US
704-864-6731		Gas-Distribution
610-832-4000		Chemicals-Specialty
713-961-4600		Steel Pipe/Tube
407-655-8000	www.quick-reilly.com	Finance-Invest Bnkr/Brkr
210-841-7600		Transport-Rail
813-573-3800	www.rjf.com	Finance-Invest Bnkr/Brkr
716-423-7270		S&L/Thrifts-Eastern US
404-586-9000		Athletic Equipment
408-262-6700	www.readrite.com	Computers-Mem Devices
608-364-8800		Mach Tools/Rel Products
423-922-1123		Theaters
914-347-7000		Medical-Biomed/Gene
612-947-7777		Retail-Hair Salons
316-727-2700	www.republic-group.com	Bldg/Construct Prod-Misc
415-780-7800	www.resound.com	Medical Products

TICKER	COMPANY NAME	ADDRESS
RESP	Respironics Inc	1001 Murry Ridge Dr, Murrysville, PA 15668
RXL	Rexel Inc	150 Alhambra Cir., Coral Gables, FL 33134
RFH	Richfood Holdings	8258 Richfood Rd., Mechanicsville,VA 23116
RIGS	Riggs National Corp Washington D.C.	1503 Pennsylvania Ave. NW, Washington, DC 20005
RIVL	Rival Co (The)	800 E. 101st Terr., Kansas City, MO 64131
RPCX	Roberts Pharm. Corp	Meridian Cntr. 2, 4 Industrial Way W., Eatontown, NJ 07724
REN	Rollins Environmental Svcs	1 Rollins Plz., Wilmington, DE 19803
RLC	Rollins Truck Leasing	1 Rollins Plz., Wilmington, DE 19803
RFED	Roosevelt Financial Group Inc	900 Roosevelt Parkway, Chesterfield, MO 63017
ROP	Roper Industries Inc	160 Ben Burton Rd., Bogart, GA 30622
ROST	Ross Stores Inc	8333 Central Ave, Newark, CA 94560
RAM	Royal Appliance Mfg	650 Alpha Dr.,Cleveland, OH 44143
RI	Ruby Tuesday Inc	4721 Morrison Dr., Mobile, AL 36609
RUS	Russ Berrie & Co Inc	111 Bauer Dr., Oakland, NJ 07436
RYAN	Ryan's Family Steak Houses Inc	405 Lancaster Avenue., Greer, SC 29650
RYK	Rykoff-Sexton Inc	613 Baltimore Dr., Wilkes-Barre, PA 18702
RYL	Ryland Group Inc	11000 Broken Land Pkwy., Columbia, MD 21044
SIII	S3 Inc	2770 San Tomas Expwy., Santa Clara, CA 95051
SFSK	Safeskin Corp	12671 High Bluff Dr., San Diego, CA 92130
SANM	Sanmina Corp	355 E. Trimble Rd., San Jose, CA 95131
SCIS	SCI Systems Inc	2101 W. Clinton Ave., Huntsville, AL 35801
SCLN	SciClone Pharm. Inc	901 Mariner's Isl. Blvd., San Mateo, CA 94404
SMG	Scotts Co (The)	14111 Scottslawn Rd., Marysville, OH 43041
SEIC	SEI Investments Co	1 Freedom Valley Dr., Oaks, PA 19456
SEI	Seitel Inc	50 Briar Hollow La., W. Bldg., Houston, TX 77027
SIGI	Selective Insur. Grp.	40 Wantage Ave., Branchville, NJ 07826
SEQU	SEQUUS Pharmaceuticals Inc	960 Hamilton Ct., Menlo Park, CA 94025
SHN	Shoney's Inc	1727 Elm Hill Pike, Nashville, TN 37210
SKO	Shopko Stores Inc	700 Pilgrim Way, Green Bay, WI 54304

PHONE	WEB ADDRESS AS OF 2/10/97	INDUSTRY SUBGROUP
412-733-0200	www.respironics.com	Respiratory Products
305-446-8000	www.rexel.com	Electronic Products-Misc
804-746-6000	www.richfood.com	Food Items-Wholesale
301-887-6000		Commer Banks-Eastrn US
816-943-4100	www.rivco.com	Appliances-Household
908-389-1182		Medical-Generic Drugs
302-426-2700		Hazardous Waste Dspsl
302-426-2700	www.rlc-corp.com	Trucking/Leasing
314-532-6200		S&L/Thrifts-Central US
706-369-7170		Miscellan.Manufactur
510-505-4400	www.rossstores.com	Retail-Apparel/Shoe
216-449-6150		Appliances-Household
334-344-3000		Retail-Restaurants
201-337-9000	www.russ-berrie.com	Consumer Products-Misc
864-879-1000		Retail-Restaurants
717-831-7500		Food Items-Wholesale
410-715-7000		Bldg-Residential/Commer
408-980-5400	www.s3.com	Elctrnc Compo-Semicon
619-794-8111		Disposable Medical Prod
408-435-8444	www.sanmina.com	Circuit Boards
205-882-4800	www.sci.com	Electronic Compo-Misc
415-358-3456	www.biospace.com/sciclone	Therapeutics
937-644-0011		Fertilizers
610-676-1000		Investment Companies
713-627-1990		Oil-Field Services
201-948-3000	www.select-ins.com	Property/Casualty Ins
415-323-9011	www.sequus.com	Medical-Drugs
615-391-5201		Retail-Restaurants
414-497-2211		Retail-Discount

TICKER	COMPANY NAME	ADDRESS
SHOR	Shorewood Packaging Corp	277 Park Ave., New York, NY 10172
SHBZ	Showbiz Pizza Time	4441 W. Airport Freeway, rving, TX 75062
SBO	Showboat Inc	2800 Fremont St., Las Vegas, NV 89104
SIE	Sierra Health Svcs.	2724 N. Tenaya Way, Las Vegas, NV 89128
SRP	Sierra Pacif. Resrcs.	6100 Neil Road, Reno, NV 89511
SMPS	Simpson Industries	47603 Halyard Dr., Plymouth, MI 48170
SKY	Skyline Corp	2520 By-Pass Rd., Elkhart, IN 46514
SKYW	Skywest Inc	444 S. River Rd., St. George, UT 84790
AOS	Smith (A.O.) Corp	11270 W. Park Pl., Milwaukee, WI 53224
SFD	Smith's Food & Drug Centers	1550 S. Redwood Road, Salt Lake City, UT 84104
SFDS	Smithfield Foods Inc	999 Waterside Dr., Norfolk, VA 23510
SNY	Snyder Oil Corp	777 Main St., Ste. 2500, Fort Worth, TX 76102
SOL	Sola Intl Inc	2420 Sand Hill Rd., Menlo Park, CA 94025
SONC	Sonic Corp	101 Park Ave., Oklahoma City, OK 73102
SCW	Southern California Water Co	630 East Foothill Blvd., San Dimas, CA 91773
SEHI	Southern Energy Homes Inc	Highway 41 North, Addison, AL 35540
SWX	Southwest Gas Corp	5241 Spring Mountain Rd., Las Vegas, NV 89193
SWN	Southwestern Energy Company	1083 Sain St., P.O.B. 1408, Fayetteville, AR 72702-1408
SVRN	Sovereign Bancorp	1130 Berkshire Blvd., Wyomissing, PA 19610
SLMD	SpaceLabs Medical	15220 NE 40th St., Redmond, WA 98052
SPAR	Spartan Motors Inc	1000 Reynolds Rd., Charlotte, MI 48813
TSA	Sports Authority Inc	3383 N. State Rd. 7, Fort Lauderdale, FL 33319
ST	SPS Technologies	101 Greenwood Ave., Jenkintown, PA 19046
SPW	SPX Corp	700 Terrace Point Dr., Muskegon, MI 49443
SJK	St John Knits Inc	17422 Derian Ave., Irvine, CA 92614
MARY	St Mary Land & Exploration Co	1776 Lincoln St., Ste. 1100, Denver, CO 80203
SPBC	St Paul Bancorp Inc	6700 W. North Ave., Chicago, IL 60707
SMSC	Standard Microsystems Corp	80 Arkay Drive, Hauppauge, NY 11788

PHONE	WEB ADDRESS AS OF 2/10/97	INDUSTRY SUBGROUP
212-371-1500		Containers-Paper/Plastic
972-258-8507		Retail-Restaurants
702-385-9123		Casino Hotels
702-242-7000		Medical-HMO
702-689-3600	www.sierrapacific.com	Electric-Integrated
313-207-6200		Auto/Trk Prts/Equip-Orig
219-294-6521		Bldg-MoblHome/MfHous
801-634-3000	www.skywest-air.com	Airlines
414-359-4000	www.aosmith.com	Auto/Trk Prts/Equip-Orig
801-974-1400		Food-Retail
757-365-3000		Food-Meat Products
817-338-4043		Oil Comp-Explor/Prodtn
415-324-6868	www.sola.com	Optical Supplies
405-280-7654	www.sonicdrivein.com	Retail-Restaurants
909-394-3600		Water
205-747-8589		Bldg-MoblHome/MfHous
702-876-7237		Gas-Distribution
501-521-1141		Gas-Distribution
610-320-8400	www.sovereignbank.com	S&L/Thrifts-Eastern US
206-882-3700	www.spacelabs.com	Patient Monitoring Equip
517-543-6400		Auto/Trk Prts/Equip-Orig
954-735-1701	www.pwr.com/SportsAuthority/	Retail-Sporting Goods
215-517-2000		Diversified Operations
616-724-5000	www.spx.com	Mach Tools/Rel Products
714-863-1171		Apparel Manufacturers
303-861-8140		Oil Comp-Explor/Prodtn
773-622-5000		S&L/Thrifts-Central US
516-435-6000	www.smc.com	Networking Products

TICKER	COMPANY NAME	ADDRESS
SMP	Standard Motor Products	37-18 Northern Blvd., Long Island City, NY 11101
SPD	Standard ProductsCo	2401 S. Gulley Rd., Dearborn, MI 48124
SPF	Standard-Pacific Crp.	1565 W. MacArthur Blvd., Costa Mesa, CA 92626
SXI	Standex Intl Corp	6 Manor Pkwy., Salem, NH 03079
STTX	Steel Technologies	15415 Shelbyville Rd., Louisville, KY 40245
SMRT	Stein Mart Inc	1200 Riverplace Blvd., Jacksonville, FL 32207
STRL	STERIS Corp	5960 Heisley Rd., Mentor, OH 44060
SSW	Sterling Software	8080 N. Central Expwy., Dallas, TX 75206
PGMS	Stillwater Mining Co	536 E. Pike Ave., Columbus, MT 59019
SW	Stone & Webster Inc	250 W. 34th St., New York, NY 10119
RGR	Sturm Ruger & Co Inc	Lacey Pl., Southport, CT 06490
BEAM	Summit Technology	21 Hickory Dr., Waltham, MA 02154
SNDT	Sungard Data Sys.	1285 Drummers La., Wayne, PA 19087
SMD	Sunrise Medical Inc	2382 Faraday Ave., Carlsbad, CA 92008
SABI	Swiss Army Brands	1 Research Dr., Shelton, CT 06484
SYB	Sybron Intl Corp	411 E. Wisconsin Ave., Milwaukee, WI 53202
SYMM	Symmetricom Inc	85 W. Tasman Dr., San Jose, CA 95134
SCOR	Syncor Intl Corp-Del	20001 Prairie St., Chatsworth, CA 91311
SSAX	System Software Associates Inc	500 W. Madison St., 32nd Fl. Chicago, IL 60661
TACO	Taco Cabana	8918 Tesoro Dr., San Antonio, TX 78217
TBCC	TBC Corp	4770 Hickory Hill Rd., Memphis, TN 38141
TBY	TCBY Enterprises Inc	425 W. Capitol Ave., Little Rock, AR 72201
TCB	TCF Financial Corp	801 Marquette Ave., Minneapolis, MN 55402
TCS	TCSI Corporation	1080 Marina Village Pkwy., Alameda, CA 94501
TECD	Tech Data Corp	5350 Tech Data Dr., Clearwater, FL 34620
TCNL	TECHNOL Medical Products Inc	7201 Industrial Park Blvd., Fort Worth, TX 76180
TLXN	Telxon Corp	3330 W. Market St., Akron, OH 44333
TNCR	Tencor Instruments	1 Technology Dr., Milpitas, CA 95035
TTRA	Tetra Technologies	25025 I-45 N., The Woodlands, TX 77380
TXI	Texas Industries Inc	1341 W. Mockingbird La., Dallas, TX 75247
THRT	Theratech Inc/Utah	417 Wakara Way, Salt Lake City, UT 84108
TII	Thomas Industries	4360 Brownsboro Rd., Louisville, KY 40207
TNM	Thomas Nelson Inc	501 Nelson Pl., Nashville, TN 37214

PHONE	WEB ADDRESS AS OF 2/10/97	INDUSTRY SUBGROUP
718-392-0200		Auto/Trk Prts/Equip-Repl
313-561-1100		Auto/Trk Prts/Equip-Orig
714-668-4300		Bldg-Residential/Commer
603-893-9701	www.standex.com	Diversified Operations
502-245-2110		Metal Processors/Fabrica
904-346-1500		Retail-Apparel/Shoe
216-354-2600		Medical Steriliz Product
214-891-8600	www.sterling.com/	Data Processing/Mgmt
303-978-2525		Precious Metals
212-290-7500	www.stoneweb.com	Building-Heavy Construct
203-259-7843	www.ruger-firearms.com	Firearms/Ammunition
617-890-1234	.	Medical Laser Systems
610-341-8700	www.sungard.com	Computer Services
619-930-1500	www.sunrisemedical.com	Hospital Beds/Equipment
203-929-6391		Consumer Products-Misc
414-274-6600	www.sybron.com	Dental Supplies/Equip
408-943-9403	www.symmetricom.com	Telecomm Equip
818-886-7400		Medical-Whsle Drug Dist
312-258-6000	www.ssax.com	Applications Software
210-804-0990		Retail-Restaurants
901-363-8030		Auto/Trk Prts/Equip-Repl
501-688-8229		Retail-Restaurants
612-661-6500		S&L/Thrifts-Central US
510-749-8500	www.tcsi.com	Communicatns Software
813-539-7429	www.techdata.com	Retail-Whsle Companies
817-581-6424		Disposable Medical Prod
330-664-1000	www.telxon.com	Computers-Micro
408-970-9500	www.tencor.com	Electric Products-Misc
281-367-1983	www.tetratec.com	Water Treatmnt Systems
972-647-6700	www.txi.com	BldgProd-Cement/Aggreg
801-588-6200	www.thrt.com	Drug Delivery Systems
502-893-4600	www.thomasind.com	Bldg Prod-Light Fixtures
615-889-9000		Publishing-Books

TICKER	COMPANY NAME	ADDRESS
THO	Thor Industries Inc	419 W. Pike St., Jackson Cntr., OH 45334
TFS	Three-Five Sys. Inc	1600 N. Desert Dr., Tempe, AZ 85281
TBL	Timberland Co	200 Domain Dr., Stratham, NH 03885
TWI	Titan Wheel Intl Inc	2701 Spruce St., Quincy, IL 62301
TJCO	TJ Intl Inc	200 E. Mallard Dr., Boise, Idaho 83706
TNP	TNP Enterprises Inc	4100 Intl. Plz., P.O.B. 2943, Fort Worth, TX 76113
TOL	Toll Brothers Inc	3103 Philmont, Huntington Valley, PA 19006
TTC	Toro Co	8111 Lyndale Ave. S., Bloomington, MN 55420
TG	Tredegar Industries	1100 Boulders Pkwy., Richmond, VA 23225
TREN	Trenwick Group Inc	Metro Cntr., 1 Station Pl., Stamford, CT 06902
TRY	Triarc Companies	280 Park Ave., New York, NY 10017
TRMB	Trimble Navigation	645 N. Mary Ave. Sunnyvale, CA 94088
TNO	True North Comms.	FCB Cntr., 101 E. Erie St., Chicago, IL 60611
TSNG	Tseng Laboratories	6 Terry Dr. Newtown, PA 18940
TUBO	Tuboscope Vetco	2835 Holmes Rd., Houston, TX 77051
TTX	Tultex Corp	101 Commonwealth Blvd, P.O.B. 5191, Martinsville, VA 24115
TTI	Tyco Toys Inc	6000 Midlantic Dr., Mt. Laurel, NJ 08054
UH	U S Home Corp	1800 West Loop S., Houston, TX 77027
UNC	UNC Inc	175 Adm. Cochrane Dr., Annapolis, MD 21401
UPC	Union Planters Corp	6200 Poplar Ave., Memphis TN 38119
UCIT	United Cities Gas Co	5300 Maryland Way, Brentwood, TN 37027
UIL	United Illuminating	157 Church St., New Haven, CT 06506
UMC	United Meridian Crp.	1201 Louisiana, Ste. 1400, Houston, TX 77002
UFPI	Universal Forest Products Inc	2801 East. Beltline NE, Grand Rapids, MI 49505
UHS	Universal Health Services	367 South Gulph Road, King of Prussia, PA 19406
UBS	US Bioscience Inc	1 Tower Bridge, 100 Front St., Ste. 24, West Conshohocken, PA 19428
USF	US Filter Corp	40-004 Cook St., Palm Desert, CA 92211
USTC	US Trust Corp	114 W. 47th St., New York, NY 10036
USAD	USA Detergents Inc	1735 Jersey Ave., North Brunswick, NJ 08902
USFC	USFreightways Corp	9700 Higgins Rd., Ste. 570, Rosemont, IL 60018
VCI	Valassis Comms. Inc	36111 Schoolcraft Rd., Livonia, MI 48150
VLNC	Valence Technology	301 Conestoga Way, Henderson, NV 89015

PHONE	WEB ADDRESS AS OF 2/10/97	INDUSTRY SUBGROUP
937-596-6849		BldgMoblHom/MfgHous
602-389-8600		Computers-Intgrtd Sys
603-772-9500		Footwear/RelatedApparel
217-228-6011		Auto/Trk Prts/Equip-Orig
208-364-3300		Bldg/Constrct Prod-Misc
817-731-0099	www.tnpe.com	Electric-Integrated
215-938-8000	www.tollbrothers.com	Bldg-Residential/Commer
612-888-8801	www.toro.com	Home Furnishings-Orig
804-330-1000	www.tredegar.com	Chemicals-Plastics
203-353-5500		Property/Casualty Ins
212-451-3000		Diversified Operations
408-481-8000	www.trimble.com	Instruments-Controls
312-751-7227		Advertising Agencies
215-968-0502	www.tseng.com	Elctrnc Compo-Semicon
713-799-5100		Oil-Field Services./Intrnatl
540-632-2961		Apparel Manufacturers
609-234-7400		Toys
713-877-1211	www.ushome.com	Bldg-Residential/Commer
410-266-7333		Aerospace/Defense-Equip
901-580-6000	www.unionplanters.com	Commer Banks-So US
615-373-5310		Gas-Distribution
203-499-2000	www.uinet.com	Electric-Integrated
713-654-9110		Oil Comp-Explor/Prodtn
616-364-6161		Bldg Prod-Wood
610-768-3300		Medical-Hospitals
610-832-0570	www.usbio.com	Therapeutics
619-340-0098	www.usfilter.com	Water Treatment Systms
212-852-1000	www.ustrust.com	Commer Banks-Eastrn US
908-828-1800		Soap/Cleaning Prepar
847-696-0200		Transport-Truck
313-591-3000		Printing-Commercial
702-558-1000		Batteries/Battery Sys

TICKER	COMPANY NAME	ADDRESS
VALM	Valmont Industries	P.O.B. 358, Valley, NE 68064
VEN	Venture Stores Inc	2001 E. Terra La., O'Fallon, MO 63366
VRTX	Vertex Pharmaceuts.	130 Waverly St., Cambridge, MA 02139
VICR	Vicor Corp	23 Frontage Rd., Andover, MA 01810
VIEW	Viewlogic Sys. Inc	293 Boston Post Rd. W, Marlboro, MA 01752
VPI	Vintage Petroleum	4200 One Williams Cntr., Tulsa, OK 74172
VISX	VISX Inc	3400 Central Expwy., Santa Clara, CA 95051
VITL	Vital Signs Inc	20 Campus Rd., Totawa, NJ 07512
VTSS	Vitesse Semicond	741 Calle Plano, Camarillo, CA 93012
V	Vivra Inc	1850 Gateway Dr., San Mateo, CA 94404
VLSI	VLSI Technology Inc	1109 McKay Dr., San Jose, CA 95131
WNC	Wabash Natl Corp	1000 Sagamore Pkwy. S., Lafayette, IN 47905
WALB	Walbro Corp	6242 Garfield St., Cass City, MI 48726
WALL	Wall Data Inc	11332 NE 122nd Way, Kirkland, WA 98034
WEG	Washington Energy	815 Mercer St., Seattle, WA 98109
WNT	Washington Natl	300 Tower Pkwy., Lincolnshire, IL 60069
WJ	Watkins-Johnson Co	3333 Hillview Ave., Palo Alto, CA 94304
WDFC	WD-40 Co	1061 Cudahy Pl., San Diego, CA 92110
WERN	Werner Enterprises Inc	14507 Frontier Road., I-80 and Highway 50, Omaha, NE 68138
WTNY	Whitney Holding Crp.	228 St. Charles Ave., New Orleans, LA 70130
WKR	Whittaker Corp	1955 N. Surveyor Ave., Simi Valley, CA 93063
WFMI	Whole Foods Mkt	601 N. Lamar, Ste. 300, Austin, TX 78703
WHX	WHX Corporation	110 E. 59th St., New York, NY 10022
WIC	Wicor Inc	626 E. Wisconsin Ave., Milwaukee, WI 53202
WSGC	Williams-Sonoma	3250 Van Ness Ave., San Francisco, CA 94109
WGO	Winnebago Industries Inc	605 West Crystal Lake Road, Forest City, IA 50436
WZR	Wiser Oil Co	8115 Preston Rd., Ste. 400, Dallas, TX 75225
WMS	WMS	3401 N. California Ave., Chicago, IL 60618
WLV	Wolverine Tube Inc	1525 Perimeter Pkwy., Huntsville, AL 35806
WWW	Wolverine World Wide Inc	9341 Courtland Dr. Rockford, MI 49351
WYL	Wyle Electronics	15370 Barranca Pkwy., Irvine, CA 92718
WN	Wynn's International	500 N. State College Blvd., Orange, CA 92868
XRIT	X-RIte Inc	3100 44th St. SW, Grandville, MI 49418

PHONE	WEB ADDRESS AS OF 2/10/97	INDUSTRY SUBGROUP
402-359-2201	www.valmont.com	Steel Pipe/Tube
314-281-5500	www.venturestores.com	Retail-Discount
617-577-6000	www.vpharm.com	Medical-Biomed/Gene
508-470-2900	www.vicr.com	Power Conv/Supply Equip
508-480-0881	www.viewlogic.com	Computer Software
918-592-0101		Oil Comp-Explor Prodtn
408-733-2020	www.visx.com	Medical Laser Systems
201-790-1330		Medical Products
805-388-3700	www.vitesse.com	Elctrnc Compo-Semicon
415-577-5700		Dialysis Centers
408-434-3000	www.vlsi.com	Elctrnc Compo-Semicon
765-448-1591	www.nlci.com/wabash	Auto-Truck Trailers
517-872-2131		Auto/Trk Prts/Equip-Orig
206-814-9255	www.walldata.com	Network Software
206-622-6767		Gas-Distribution
847-793-3000		Life/Health Insurance
415-493-4141	www.wj.com	Elctrnc Compo-Semicon
619-275-1400		Paint/Related Products
402-895-6640	www.werner.com	Transport-Truck
504-586-7117		Commer Banks-So US
805-526-5700	www.whittaker.com	Electric Products-Misc
512-477-4455	www.wholefoods.com	Food-Retail
212-355-5200		Steel-Producers
414-291-7026		Gas-Distribution
415-421-7900		Retail-Mail Order
515-582-3535	www.winnebagoind.com	Bldg-MoblHome/MfHous
214-265-0080		Oil Comp- Explor/Prodtn
773-961-1111	www.wms.com/williams/	Leisure/Rec/ Gaming
205-353-1310		Metal Processors/Fabrica
616-866-5500		Footwear/RelatedApparel
714-753-9953	www.wyle.com	Electronic Parts Distrib
714-938-3700		Auto/Trk Prts/Equip-Repl
616-534-7663	www.xrite.com	Instruments-Controls

TICKER	COMPANY NAME	ADDRESS
XIRC	Xircom Inc	2300 Corp. Cntr. Dr., Thousand Oaks, CA 91320
YELL	Yellow Corp	10990 Roe Ave., Overland Park, KS 66211
ZBRA	Zebra Technologies	333 Corp. Woods Pkwy., Vernon Hills, IL 60061
ZNT	Zenith Nat. Insur. Cp	21255 Califa St., Woodland Hills, CA 91367
ZRO	Zero Corp-Del	444 S. Flower St., Los Angeles, CA 90071
ZLG	Zilog Inc	210 E. Hacienda Ave, Campbell, CA 95008
ZION	Zions Bancorporation	1 S. Main St., Salt Lake City, UT 84111
ZOLL	Zoll Medical Corp	32 Second Ave., Burlington, MA 01803

PHONE	WEB ADDRESS AS OF 2/10/97	INDUSTRY SUBGROUP
805-376-9300	www.xircom.com	Networking Products
913-696-6100	www.yellowfreight.com/	Transport-Truck
847-634-6700	www.zebra.com	Printers/Related Prod
818-713-1000	www.zic.com	Multi-line Insurance
213-629-7000	www.zerocorp.com	Containers-Metal/Glass
408-370-8000	www.zilog.com	Elctrnc Compo-Semicond
801-524-4787	www.zionsbank.com	Commer Banks-WestrnUS
617-229-0020		Medical Instruments

SMALL-CAPS
State by State

HERE IS A STATE BY STATE directory to the companies in the first part of this Appendix.

ALABAMA

Birmingham Steel Corp
Books-A-Million Inc
Energen Corp
Kinder-Care Learning Centers
Protective Life Corp
Ruby Tuesday Inc
SCI Systems Inc
Southern Energy Homes Inc
Wolverine Tube Inc

ARIZONA

Aztar Corp
Bell Sports Corp
Continental Homes Holding
MicroAge Inc
Microchip Technology Inc
Three-Five Systems Inc

ARKANSAS

Acxiom Corp
American Freightways Corp
Arkansas Best Corp
Baldor Electric
First Commercial Corp

Southwestern Energy Company
TCBY Enterprises Inc

BERMUDA

Mutual Risk Management LTD

CALIFORNIA

ABM Industries Inc
ADAC Laboratories
Advanced Tissue Sciences Inc
Alliance Pharmaceutical Cp
Ashworth Inc
Aspect Telecommunications
Auspex Systems Inc
Authentic Fitness Corp
Bell Industries Inc
Benton Oil & Gas Co
Boole & Babbage Inc
Broderbund Software Inc
BW/IP Inc
Calgene Inc
California Microwave
Centigram Communications
Cheesecake Factory (The)
Chips & Technologies Inc

Circon Corp

CKE Restaurant Inc

Coast Savings Financial Inc

Coherent Inc

Collagen Corp

Compression Labs

COR Therapeutics Inc

Custom Chrome Inc

Cygnus Inc

Dames & Moore Inc

Digital Microwave Corp

Dionex Corp

Downey Financial Corp

Etec Systems Inc

Fair Issac & Company Inc

Fidelity National Finl Inc

Filenet Corp

First American Finl

Foodmaker Inc

Fremont General Corp

Fritz Companies Inc

Galoob Toys Inc

Gottschalks Inc

Hollywood Park Inc

HS Resources Inc

IHOP Corp

Immune Response Corp/Del

Intl Rectifier Corp

K-Swiss Inc

K2 Inc

Komag Inc

Logicon Inc

Mail Boxes Etc

Marshall Industries

Mentor Corp

Molecular Biosystems Inc

Mycogen Corp

Network Equipment Tech Inc

Network General Corp

North American Mortgage

Novellus Systems Inc

NTN Communications Inc

Pacific Scientific Co

Platinum Software Corp

Protein Design Labs Inc

Read-Rite Corp

Resound Corp

Ross Stores Inc

S3 Inc

Safeskin Corp

Sanmina Corp

SciClone Pharmaceuticals Inc

SEQUUS Pharmaceuticals Inc

Sola International Inc

Southern California Water Co

St John Knits Inc

Standard-Pacific Corp

Sunrise Medical Inc

Symmetricom Inc

Syncor Intl Corp-Del

TCSI Corporation

Tencor Instruments

Trimble Navigation Ltd

US Filter Corp

VISX Inc

Vitesse Semiconductor Corp

Vivra Inc

VLSI Technology Inc

Watkins-Johnson Company

WD-40 Co

Whittaker Corp

Williams-Sonoma Inc

Wyle Electronics

Wynn's International Inc

CALIFORNIA (CONT.)

Xircom Inc
Zenith National Insurance Cp
Zero Corp-Del
Zilog Inc

CANADA

Cineplex Odeon Corporation
Glamis Gold Ltd

COLORADO

American Medical Response
Barrett Resources Corp
Commnet Cellular Inc
Getchell Gold Corp
Hauser Inc
K N Energy Inc
MDC Holdings Inc
St Mary Land & Exploration

CONNECTICUT

ADVO Inc
Air Express International Cp
Aquarion Co
Connecticut Energy Corp
Ethan Allen Interiors Inc
Gerber Scientific Inc
Hyperion Software Corp
Kaman Corp
Landstar System Inc
Life Re Corp
Lone Star Industries
Lydall Inc
Mariner Health Group Inc
NFO Research Inc
Sturm Ruger & Co Inc
Swiss Army Brands Inc

Trenwick Group Inc
United Illuminating Co

DELAWARE

Rollins Environmental Svcs
Rollins Truck Leasing Corp

WASHINGTON DC

Riggs Natl Corp Wash D C

FLORIDA

American Bankers Insur Group
BE Aerospace Inc
Breed Technologies Inc
Catalina Marketing Corp
Discount Auto Parts
Hughes Supply Inc
Interim Services Inc
Jan Bell Marketing Inc
Jumbosports Inc
Levitz Furniture Inc
Lincare Holdings Inc
Noven Pharmaceuticals Inc
Photronics Inc
Quick & Reilly Group Inc
Raymond James Financial Corp
Rexel Inc
Sports Authority Inc
Stein Mart Inc
Tech Data Corp

GEORGIA

AGCO Corp
Caraustar Industries Inc
Carmike Cinemas Inc
Compdent Corporation
GranCare Inc

Greenfield Industries Inc

Interface Inc

Johnston Ind-Del

Kuhlman Corp

Magellan Health Services

Mohawk Industries Inc

National Data Corp

Norrell Corp

Oxford Industries Inc

Paragon Trade Brands Inc

RDM Sports Group Inc

Roper Industries Inc

IDAHO

BMC West Corp

Coeur D'alene Mines Corp

Hecla Mining Co

Morrison Knudsen Corp

TJ International Inc

ILLINOIS

Aar Corp

Acme Metals Inc

Amcol International Corp

Anixter International Inc

Aptargroup Inc

Castle (A.M.) & Co

Cilcorp Inc

Clarcor Inc

Dekalb Genetics Corp

Devry Inc

Gallagher (Arthur J.) & Co

Hartmarx Corp

Insurance Auto Auctions Inc

Juno Lighting Inc

Material Sciences Corp

McWhorter Technologies Inc

Methode Electronics

Northwestern Steel & Wire Co

Outboard Marine Corp

Platinum Technology Inc

Premark International Inc

St Paul Bancorp Inc

System Software Assoc Inc

Titan Wheel Intl Inc

True North Communications

USFreightways Corporation

Washington Natl Corp

WMS Industries Inc

Zebra Technologies Corp

INDIANA

Lilly Industries Inc

Skyline Corp

Wabash National Corp

IOWA

Allied Group Inc

Casey's General Stores Inc

Heartland Express Inc

Interstate Power Co

Norand Corp

Winnebago Industries

KANSAS

Angelica Corp

Applebees Intl Inc

Republic Gypsum Co

Yellow Corporation

KENTUCKY

Commonwealth Aluminum Corp

Steel Technologies Inc

Thomas Industries Inc

LOUISIANA

Offshore Logistics

MAINE

Bangor Hydro-Electric Co

Consumers Water Co

IDEXX Laboratories Inc

MARYLAND

Alex Brown Inc

Hechinger Co

Integrated Health Services

Legg Mason Inc

MedImmune Inc

North American Vaccine Inc

Ryland Group Inc

UNC Inc

MASSACHUSETTS

Au Bon Pain Co Inc

Baker (J.) Inc

Banyan Systems Inc

BBN Corp

Bertucci's, Inc

Cognex Corp

Commonwealth Energy System

Cyrk International Inc

Designs Inc

Dynatech Corp

Eastern Utilities Assoc

Eaton Vance Corp

Filene's Basement Corp

GC Companies Inc

Immulogic Pharmaceutical

Ionics Inc

Keane Inc

Kronos Inc

Microcom Inc

New England Business Svc Inc

Oak Industries Inc.

PerSeptive Biosystems Inc

PictureTel Corp

Pioneer Group Inc

Primark Corp

Progress Software Corp

Summit Technology Inc

Vertex Pharmaceuticals Inc

Vicor Corp

Viewlogic Systems Inc

Zoll Medical Corp

MICHIGAN

Arbor Drugs Inc

Champion Enterprises Inc

Core Industries Inc

First Michigan Bank Corp

Gentex Corp

Intermet Corp

Kysor Industrial Corp

La-Z-Boy Inc

Simpson Industries

Spartan Motors Inc

SPX Corp

Standard Products Co

Universal Forest Products

Valassis Communications Inc

Walbro Corp

Wolverine World Wide

X-Rite Inc

MINNESOTA

Alliant Techsystems Inc

Apogee Enterprises Inc

Arctic Cat Inc

BMC Industries Inc-Minn

Control Data Systems Inc

Damark International Inc -A

Digi International Inc

G & K Services Inc

Grand Casinos Inc

Interra Financial Inc

Merrill Corporation

Nash Finch Co

National Computer Sys Inc

Patterson Dental Company

Piper Jaffrey Funds

Regis Corp

TCF Financial Corp

Toro Co

MISSISSIPPI

Casino Magic Corp

Chem First Inc

Deposit Guaranty Corp

Mississippi Chemical Corp

MISSOURI

Brown Group Inc

Butler Mfg Co

Cerner Corp

Earthgrains Company

Express Scripts Inc

Harmon Industries Inc

Henry (Jack) & Associates

Interstate Bakeries

Kellwood Co

Magna Group Inc

Mark Twain Bancshares Inc

O'Reilly Automotive Inc

Payless Cashways Inc

Rival Co (The)

Roosevelt Financial Grp Inc

Venture Stores Inc

MONTANA

Stillwater Mining Company

NEBRASKA

Commercial Federal Corp

Lindsay Manufacturing Co

Valmont Industries

Werner Enterprises Inc

NEVADA

Mesa Air Group Inc

Showboat Inc

Sierra Health Services

Sierra Pacific Resources

Southwest Gas Corp

Valence Technology Inc

NEW HAMPSHIRE

Fisher Scientific Intl

Nashua Corp

Standex International Corp

Timberland Company

NEW JERSEY

Air & Water Tech

Alpharma Inc

BISYS Group Inc

Cambrex Corp

Collective Bancorp Inc

Fedders Corp

Geotek Communications Inc

IMO Industries Inc

J & J Snack Foods Corp

KCS Energy Inc

NEW JERSEY (CONT.)

Lechters Inc
Liposome Company Inc
New Jersey Resources
Players International Inc
Prime Hospitality Corp
Roberts Pharmaceutical Corp
Russ Berrie & Co Inc
Selective Insurance Group
Tyco Toys Inc
USA Detergents Inc
Vital Signs Inc

NEW YORK

Astoria Financial Corp
Bowne & Co Inc
Capital Re Corp
Central Hudson Gas & Elec
Comverse Technology Inc
Dress Barn Inc
Enhance Financial Svcs Group
Enzo Biochem Inc
Frontier Insurance Group Inc
Galey & Lord Inc
Griffon Corporation
Handy & Harman
Intermagnetics General Corp
JSB Financial Inc
Lillian Vernon Corp
Nautica Enterprises Inc
NBTY Inc
ONBANCorp Inc
Orange & Rockland Utilities
Orion Capital Corp
Park Electrochemical Corp
PAXAR Corp
Pharmaceutical Marketing Svs

Pharmaceutical Resources Inc
Phillips-Van Heusen
Plenum Publishing Corp
PLY GEM Industries
RCSB Financial Inc
Regeneron Pharmaceutical
Shorewood Packaging Corp
Standard Microsystems Corp
Standard Motor Prods
Stone & Webster Inc
Triarc Companies
US Trust Corp
WHX Corporation

NORTH CAROLINA

Broadband Technologies Inc
Cato Corp
CCB Financial Corp
Centura Banks Inc
Coca-Cola Bottling
Cone Mills Corp
Fieldcrest Cannon
Goodmark Foods
Guilford Mills Inc
Insteel Industries
Integon Corp/Del
Oakwood Homes
Piedmont Natural Gas Co
Public Service Co Of N C

OHIO

Allen Group
Amcast Indl Corp
Charter One Fin Inc
Chemed Corp
Chiquita Brands Intl
Comair Holdings Inc

Fabri-Centers Of America
Figgie International
FirstMerit Corporation
Geon Company
Huffy Corp
Invacare Corp
Medusa Corp
Myers Industries Inc
National Auto Credit Inc
OHM Corp
OM Group Inc
Omnicare Inc
Pioneer Standard Electronics
Provident Bancorp Inc
Royal Appliance Mfg Co
Scotts Company (The)
STERIS Corp
Telxon Corp
Thor Industries Inc

OKLAHOMA

Devon Energy Corporation
Liberty Bancorp Inc/Oklahoma
LSB Industries Inc
Sonic Corp
Vintage Petroleum Inc
Whitney Holding Corp

OREGON

Lattice Semiconductor Corp
Northwest Natural Gas Co
Pope & Talbot Inc

PENNSYLVANIA

C-COR Electronics
CDI Corp
Cephalon Inc

CMAC Investment Corp
Dravo Corp
Genesis Health Ventures
Integrated Circuit Systems
Keystone Fin Inc
Penn Enterprises Inc
Philadelphia Suburban Corp
Quaker Chemical Corp
Respironics Inc
Rykoff-Sexton Inc
SEI Investments Co
Sovereign Bancorp Inc
SPS Technologies Inc
Sungard Data Systems Inc
Toll Brothers Inc
Tseng Laboratories Inc
Universal Health Services
US Bioscience Inc

PUERTO RICO

FirstBank Puerto Rico

RHODE ISLAND

Cross (A.T.) Company

SOUTH CAROLINA

Delta Woodside Inds Inc
KEMET Corp
Ryan's Family Stk Houses Inc

TENNESSEE

Astec Industries Inc
Corrections Corp Of America
Coventry Corporation
Dixie Yarns Inc
Envoy Corporation
Insituform Technologies Inc

TENNESSEE (CONT.)

MS Carriers Inc

Mueller Industries Inc

PhyCor Inc

Proffitts Inc

Regal Cinemas Inc

Shoney's Inc

TBC Corp

Thomas Nelson Inc

Union Planters Corp

United Cities Gas Co

TEXAS

Allwaste Inc

Amresco Inc

Amtech Corp

Atmos Energy Corp

BancTec Inc

Benchmark Electronics Inc

Bombay Company Inc (The)

Box Energy Corp

Cabot Oil & Gas Corp

Camco International Inc

Cash America Investments Inc

Commercial Metals Co

CompUSA Inc

Cross Timbers Oil Co

Cullen/Frost Bankers Inc

Cyrix Corp

Dallas Semiconductor Corp

Daniel Industries

Fibreboard Corp

Frozen Food Express Inds

Global Industries Tech Inc

Haggar Corp

IMCO Recycling Inc

Input/Output Inc

Intervoice Inc

Justin Industries

Kent Electronics Corp

Kirby Corp

Living Centers of America

Luby's Cafeterias Inc

Mesa Inc

Michaels Stores Inc

Newfield Exploration Company

Noble Drilling Corp

Oceaneering Intl Inc

Pier 1 Imports Inc-Del

Pillowtex Corp

Plains Resources Inc

Pogo Producing Co

Pool Energy Services Co

Pride Petroleum Svcs Inc

Production Operators Corp

Quanex Corp

Railtex Inc

Seitel Inc

Showbiz Pizza Time Inc

Snyder Oil Corp

Sterling Software Inc

Taco Cabana

Tetra Technologies Inc

Texas Industries Inc

TNP Enterprises Inc

Tuboscope Vetco Intl Corp

U S Home Corp

United Meridian Corp

Whole Foods Market Inc

Wiser Oil Co

Tecnol Medical Products Inc

UTAH

Ballard Medical Products

Franklin Quest Co

Natures Sunshine Prods Inc

Skywest Inc

Smith's Food & Drug Ctrs

Theratech Inc/Utah

Zions Bancorporation

VERMONT

Central Vermont Pub Serv

Green Mountain Power Corp

VIRGINIA

American Management Systems

Bassett Furniture Inds

Dimon Inc

Hilb, Rogal & Hamilton Co

Intl Family Entertainment

O'Sullivan Corp

Orbital Sciences Corp

Owens & Minor Inc Hldg Co

Pittston Burlington Group

Richfood Holdings Inc

Smithfield Foods Inc

Tredegar Industries Inc

Tultex Corp

WASHINGTON

Cascade Natural Gas Corp

CellPro Inc

Eagle Hardware & Garden

Expeditors Intl Wash Inc

Flow Intl Corp

Fluke Corp

Itron Inc

Omega Environmental Inc

Penwest Ltd

SpaceLabs Medical Inc

Wall Data Inc

Washington Energy Co

WISCONSIN

Carson Pirie Scott & Co

First Fin Corp -Wisc

Manitowoc Co

Marcus Corp

Mosinee Paper Corp

Oshkosh B'gosh Inc

Plexus Corp

Regal Beloit

Shopko Stores Inc

Smith (A.O.) Corp

Sybron Intl Corp

Wicor Inc

About Bloomberg

Bloomberg Financial Markets is a global, multimedia-based distributor of information services, combining news, data, and analysis for financial markets and businesses. Bloomberg carries real-time pricing, data, history, analytics, and electronic communications that is available 24 hours a day and is currently accessed by 200,000 financial professionals in 91 countries.

Bloomberg covers all key global securities markets, including equities, money markets, currencies, municipals, corporate/euro/sovereign bonds, commodities, mortgage-backed securities, derivative products, and governments. The company also delivers access to Bloomberg News, whose more than 400 reporters and editors in 70 bureaus worldwide provide around-the-clock coverage of economic, financial, and political events.

The company information in the Appendix of this book was provided by Bloomberg's **Equity Department**, which maintains detailed current data and analytic functions on over 60,000 companies in 80 countries.

To learn more about Bloomberg—one of the world's fastest-growing real-time financial information networks—call a sales representative at:

Frankfurt:	49-69-920-410
Hong Kong:	852-2521-3000
London:	44-171-330-7500
New York:	1-212-318-2000
Princeton:	1-609-279-3000
São Paulo:	5511-3048-4500
Singapore:	65-226-3000
Sydney:	61-2-9777-8600
Tokyo:	81-3-3201-8900

About the Authors

Christopher Graja is senior markets editor for *Bloomberg: A Magazine for Market Professionals* and for *Bloomberg Personal* magazine. He holds an MBA from Rutgers University and was the director of training and a senior researcher for Bloomberg L.P.'s research division.

Mr. Graja welcomes reader comments and suggestions for future editions of this book. He may be reached by mail in care of Bloomberg Press, P.O. Box 888, Princeton, NJ 08542-0888, or via email at smallcap@bloomberg.com.

Elizabeth Ungar, Ph.D., is author of *Swap Literacy: A Comprehensible Guide*, published by Bloomberg Press. She has taught at Trinity College, Dublin, and is a senior editor of both *Bloomberg Personal* and *Bloomberg: A Magazine for Market Professionals*, in which she regularly converts highly technical subjects into highly readable prose. She has worked for *Business Month; Manhattan,inc.; Institutional Investor,* and *American Banker.* Ms. Ungar edited *An Introduction to Option-Adjusted Spread Analysis,* by Tom Windas, published by Bloomberg Professional Library.